以认知理论
进行汉语连动式结构的研究

A Cognitive Approach to
Serial Verb Constructions in Mandarin Chinese

印辉 著

厦门大学出版社
XIAMEN UNIVERSITY PRESS

国家一级出版社
全国百佳图书出版单位

［基金项目］

本书为厦门理工学院社会科学研究

项目（YSK11005R）研究成果，并获

该项目经费资助

Abstract

This study aims at solving a long-standing problem in Mandarin linguistics, namely how to categorize and understand the plethora of constructions that have been called SVCs (Serial Verb Constructions) at one time or another. This study examines features which differentiate them from typical cases of coordination, subordination. It demonstrates that the main differences between SVCs and non-SVCs lie in their different profiles. My classification for an SVC is based on the three iconically based semantic principles: **temporal sequence** and **scope**, **shared participants**, and **situational dependence**. Grounded on these three principles, seven morphosyntactic and prosodic tests have been proposed to apply to five constructions which consist of more than one verb. The seven operational iconic/semantic tests allow us to capture common features of SVCs in Mandarin Chinese. Mandarin SVCs reflect cognitive packaging, that is, an SVC denotes a unitary complex event and reflects event conflation of two or more sub-events. The five constructions reflect degrees of serialization or a continuum of event conflation in Mandarin. In this study, two experiments were designed to explore the phenomenon of event autonomy or event conflation of the five [V (N) V ...] types and the effects of construal on the interpretation of different constructions. The findings in the experiments suggest that Mandarin speakers are sensitive to sentences exhibiting different degrees of event conflation. The results in the experiments indicate that event conflation really turned out to be a graded rather than a discrete phenomenon. The phenomena of Mandarin SVCs provide evidence for a kind of iconicity operating in the coding of multi-verb structures.

This study explores the Lancaster Corpus of Mandarin Chinese for multi-verb constructions (MVCs) containing two or more verbs in a sequence. The corpus results indicate that there is a delicate interaction between lexical items and the construction types they enter into. Certain verbs are easily attracted to a particular construction or even a particular verb position. The results also suggest that there are degrees of freedom and fixedness in the collocating verbs associated with different multi-verb constructions.

By providing a fine-grained analysis of a central feature of Mandarin grammar this research not only provides insight into Chinese linguistics, but also advances the discussion of the graded phenomenon in language. The experimental components show the relevance of perspective or construal on the interpretation of language and the effects of conceptualization on grammatical structures. Thus, this study supports central claims in cognitive linguistics and provides an empirically valid account for the connection between language and cognition.

List of Abbreviations

PERF: perfective

PROG: progressive

EXP: experiential

LOC: locative

PRES: present

CL: classifier

1SG: first person singular

1PL: first person plural

2SG: second person singular

3SG: third person singular

3SGF: third person singular female

3SGM: third person singular male

PL: plural

PRT: particle

NEG: negation

INJ: interjection

POSS: possessive

BA: object marker in the *ba*-construction

BEI: passive marker in the *bei*-construction

OBJ: object marker

RC: relative clause marker

ASP: aspectual marker

Contents

Chapter One

Introduction

Mandarin Chinese is classified as an isolating and non-inflecting language. What English achieves by changing verb forms is expressed in Mandarin Chinese by means of additional adverbs, other independent morphemes, etc. For example, in Mandarin *lai* ' come ' remains the same morphologically no matter when the action happened or happens or will happen since Mandarin does not inflect its verbs for tenses (Lin 2001). In syntax, Mandarin has very few overt morphosyntactic expressions of tense or aspect and has no subject-verb agreement, in contrast to inflectional languages. The lack of affixational morphology and syntactic markers in Chinese often makes a string of words highly ambiguous syntactically and, thus, a Mandarin expression with two or more verbs in a sequence could be associated with more than one construction type. For example, a multi-verb sequence in Mandarin could be analyzed as coordination (not unlike the English expression *eat* [and] *drink*), subordination (as in the English *I want* [to] *go*), or causation (such as *I made him leave*). A "multi-verb expression" is understood as a sequence of verbs (with a shared or omitted participant) in an expression without any syntactic marking to indicate what the relation is between the verbs.

Serial verb constructions (SVCs) are prevalent in Mandarin Chinese and deserve more investigation than they have thus far received. In the past, different linguists have given different classifications to multi-verb expressions with shared subjects. The string [NP V (NP) V ...] is at least 5-way ambiguous in Mandarin (with the optional inter-verbal NP functioning either as matrix DO or embedded SUBJ), as shown in the following labeled examples:

(1) COORDINATED CLAUSE CONSTRUCTION

Ta　　meitian　**duanlain**　(ta)　(meitian)　**xuexi**　yingyu.

3SG　everyday　**exercise**　(3SG)(everyday)　**study**　English

'S/he exercises and studies English everyday.'

(2) CLAUSAL COMPLEMENT CONSTRUCTION

Ta　　**chengren**　(ta)　　**zuo** cuo　　le.

3SG　**confess**　(3SG)　**do** wrong　ASP

'S/he confessed that s/he had done something wrong.'

(3) PURPOSIVE COMPLEMENT CONSTRUCTION

Ta　　**mai**　piao　**kan**　dianying.

3SG　**buy**　ticket　**see**　film

'S/he bought a ticket to see a film.'

(4) DOUBLE-HEADED/SHARED OBJECT CONSTRUCTION

Ta　　**zhong**　cai　　**mai.**

3SG　**plant**　vegetable　**sell**

'S/he planted vegetables to sell.'

(5) VV COMPOUND CONSTRUCTION

Ta　　**tui**　**dao** le　wo.

3SG　**push**　**fall** ASP　I

'S/he pushed me down.'

Each of the constructions in (1) to (5) has been labeled an SVC at one time or another. As is apparent, there are no agreed-upon criteria for either what is or is not an SVC or for sub-classifications within the SVC category as a whole. Previous analyses have fallen short mainly because they either are based on syntactic criteria which are overtly exclusive or fail to explain why verb serialization is so robust in Mandarin. The aim of this study is to integrate past examples and provide an operative and unified account for what is and what is not an SVC in Mandarin. It will be demonstrated that this aim can be achieved through the present analysis which takes a cognitive/functional perspective. Based on such an approach, SVCs will be characterized as follows. SVCs refer to two or more events which exhibit some degree of semantic interdependence — a purposive or causal relationship. They involve the integration of two or more events into one macro event or they are understood to be related as parts (or phases) of one overall event. These events are denoted by two or more verbal phrases without any syntactic marker between them. The more interdependence or integrated the two events, the better an SVC. As expected, the classification in this study is based on a set of iconically based semantic principles, which can characterize all true SVCs in Mandarin Chinese.

Chapter Two

Past Treatments of Serial Verb Constructions

In this chapter, I will first survey past treatments of verb serialization in general, and then I will discuss past approaches to Chinese SVCs in particular. After the literature of serial verb constructions has been reviewed, it will become apparent that there is little consensus about what is or is not an SVC.

2.1 *Past Approaches to SVCs*

The phenomenon of serialized verbs was first described more than a hundred years ago by Christaller (1875). However, extensive and intensive formal syntactic research began to be conducted only after the publication of Chomsky's *Syntactic Structures* in the late 1950s (Stewart 2001). Since then, various approaches to SVCs have been adopted to account for the phenomenon. Nevertheless, Stewart (2001 : 3) claims that after "over one century of grammatical analysis the SVC is still an ill-defined and often misinterpreted phenomenon ". The following are representative studies that have dealt with the phenomenon of SVCs.

2.1.1 *Christaller* (1875)

Christaller (1875) was the first known scholar to have studied SVCs from a grammatical perspective. In his book, *A Grammar of the Asante and Fante Language called Tshi*, he states that it is possible for two or more verbs, which are not connected by conjunctions, to have the same subject in a Twi (Tshi) sentence. He distinguishes two basic types of verb combinations: essential combinations and accidental combinations.

By essential combinations, he refers to a construction in which one verb is principal and the other verb is an auxiliary verb which supplies an adverb of time or manner, or forms a complement or adjunct. The second verb is generally a supplemental verb which forms a part of a larger verbal phrase (Christaller 1875). The actions expressed by the two verbs are simultaneous and the two are in an internal or inseparable relation or connection. In these cases, the auxiliary or supplemental verb is coordinate only in form, but subordinate in sense, as in the following examples:

(6) a. *Oguare*　　　　*baa*　　　　　*mpoano.*

　　　he. swim. PAST　come. PAST　shore

　　　'He swam to the shore. '　　　(Christaller 1875: 144)

　　b. *Oyɛ*　　　　adwuma　　　man　　　ne　　nan.

　　　he. do. PRES　*work*　　　*give. PRES*　*his*　　*mother*

　　　'He works for his mother. '　　(*Christaller* 1875: 144)

As for accidental combinations, Christaller (1875: 143-4) *indicates that two or more predicates (verbs with or without complements or adjuncts) which express different successive actions or denote a state simultaneous with another state or action happen to have the same subject and are merely joined together without conjunction. In accidental combinations, two or more sentences are contracted into one and the two verbs are coordinate in sense as well as in form, as exemplified in* (7) (*cf. Sebba* 1987):

(7) *a.* Osoree　　　　guaree　　　srae.

　　　he. arise. PAST　wash. PAST　anoint. PAST

　　　'He arose, washed (and) anointed himself. '

　　　　　　　　　　　　　　　　(*Christaller* 1875: 144)

　　b. Yesoree　　　　ntem　　koo　　　ofie.

　　　we. arise. PAST　*quick*　*go. PAST*　*home*

'We arose quickly (and) went home. '

(Christaller 1875: 144)

Obviously, Christaller's analysis of SVCs is consonant with the traditional classification of verb combinations, which claims that the relationship of verb combinations is either one of coordination or subordination. His accidental combinations of verbs are commonly referred to by other linguists as " coordinate SVCs" while essential combinations of verbs as " subordinate SVCs". Interestingly, Christaller implies that two or more sentences underlie a coordinate SVC. Chen (1993) claims that this view still holds in the modern linguistic literature.

2.1.2 Westermann (1930)

Another linguist who provides detailed descriptions of SVCs in West African languages is Westermann (1930). In his study of the Ewe language, he does not classify SVCs into either coordinate constructions or subordinate constructions as Christaller does. He states that a row of verbs often occur one after another. The main features of such verb sequences are that all the verbs stand next to each other without being connected, that all have the same tense or mood, and that in the event of their having a common subject and object, these surface near the first verb while the others remain bare. In case a conjunction should stand between the two verbs, the subject and object must be repeated. It seems to Westermann that the sentence in (8a) is a case of an SVC, but that the one in (8b) is not, since (8b) features a conjunction between the two verbs.

(8) *a.* etsɔa　　　　îu.

　　　 he. took. it　　ate

　　　 ' He took it (and) ate it.　　　　　　(Chen 1993: 4)

　　 b. etsɔa　　　eye　　wo îui.

　　　 he. took. it　and　　he. ate. it

' He took it and he ate it. '   (*Chen* 1993 : 4)

In addition , Westermann describes a type of idiom which contains two verbs in a series. He claims that this type of idiom is a variation of an SVC in Ewe. He states that mostly the two verbs are conjugated in the same way as in (9 *a*) ; *however, occasionally the second verb is not conjugated , as in* (9 *b*).

(9) *a.* maxɔ   nya   la   ase.

　　　I. will. accept   word   the   will. hear

　　　' I will believe in a word. '   (*Chen* 1993 : 4)

　　b. mexɔ   nya   la   se.

　　　I. accepted   word   the   hear

　　　' I believed in a word. '   (*Chen* 1993 : 4)

Both Christaller (1875) *and Westermann* (1930) *provide details of SVCs in African languages although neither does more than describe the phenomenon* (*Chen* 1993). *Neither of them is concerned with grammatical or theoretical issues such as why a sentence has more than one verb. Their main concern is to write pedagogical grammars that could facilitate the interaction between native speakers of West African languages and foreigners. Since these early investigators first described SVCs in West African languages, the general impression used to be that serial verb phenomena were localized to the languages of West Africa* (*Stewart* 2001).

2.1.3 Stewart (1963)

With regard to SVCs, matters changed with the dawn of generative grammar (*Chomsky* 1957) *and accounts of SVCs went from purely descriptive to more theoretical, especially taking a transformational flavor. Chomsky's book,* Syntactic Structures, *formalizes the description of a sentence in terms of the notion of a set of Phrase Structure Rules that characterize linguistic competence and serve as the underlying base from which all surface constructions in a language are generated. The basic idea concerning underlying sentence structure is that a clause has only one main verb or, put another way, a clause contains only one finite verb. The view that one clause allows only one finite verb made serial verb phenomena sound like some kind of oddity (Stewart 2001). However, generative grammarians claimed that through the power of transformations, the problem of a finite clause containing more than one verb could be solved.*

Stewart (1963) is credited with the first generative analysis of SVCs. He suggests that generative grammar can create structures and then delete portions of them by transformations when certain conditions are met. He assumes that an SVC sentence is formed from two or more underlying clauses. He proposes that the sentence in (10) in the Twi language is derived from the two underlying or deep structure mono-clausal sentences shown in (11a) and (11b).

(10) Akorɔma   no   kyeree   akokɔ   no   wee.

    hawk   *that*   *caught*   *chicken*   *that*   *ate*

    '*The hawk caught the chicken (and) ate (it).*'

                             (*Stewart* 1963: 145)

(11) *a.* Akor ɔma   no   kyeree   akokɔ   no.

      hawk   *that*   *caught*   *chicken*   *that*

      '*The hawk caught the chicken*'   (*Stewart* 1963: 145)

   b. Akorɔma   no   wee   akokɔ   no.

      hawk   *that*   *ate*   *chicken*   *that*

      '*The hawk ate the chicken.*'   (*Stewart* 1963: 145)

Stewart proposes two transformations to derive the sentence in (10) from the two underlying sentences in (11): the subject transformation (deletion) indicated in (12) and the object transformation (deletion) indicated in (13) (Stewart 1963: 145).

(12) *SUBJECT DELETION*:

    The subject, which must be the same in each of the underlying simple sentences if they are to be eligible for coordination in a serial verbal sentence, is generally deleted in each sentence other than the first.

(13) *OBJECT DELETION:*

If two or more successive underlying sentences have the same direct object, this direct object is deleted in each of the sentences other than the first in which it occurs.

Stewart is mainly concerned with how to account for the missing subjects and missing objects when two transitive verbs happen to occur in a single sentence. He assumes that transformations are able to delete recoverable subjects and objects and, thus, can generate such constructions when two verbs appear in a sequence in surface structure.

2.1.4 Bamgbose (1974)

Bamgbose's (1974) main interests are in establishing different kinds of serial verbs based on the relations between them. He identifies two types of SVCs in Yoruba, another West Africa language: the linking type and the modifying type. He assumes that these two types are different from each other in that only SVCs of the linking type are derived from two or more underlying sentences through transformations, while those of the modifying type are not.

He argues that the sentence in (14), an SVC of the linking type, is derived from the two underlying clauses shown in (15a) and (15b).

(14) mo   mu   iwe   wa   ile.

　　　I　　took　book　come　home

　　　'I brought a book home'.　　　　　(*Bamgbose* 1974: 19)

(15) a. mo mu   iwe.

　　　　I　took　book

　　　　'I took a book.'　　　　　　　　(*Bamgbose* 1974: 19)

　　　b. mo si   wa   ile.

　　　　I　and　came　home.

　　　　'and I came home.'　　　　　　(*Bamgbose* 1974: 19)

Bamgbose's SVCs of the linking type seem to correspond to coordinate constructions in traditional analyses. The traditional view about the derivation of coordinate constructions through transformations still holds in the present literature (Chen 1993).

As for SVCs of the modifying type, in Bamgbose's view they are not derived from two or more underlying sentences. He claims that any transformation starting from two separate sentences/clauses to derive SVCs of the modifying type would involve meaning change. For example, he claims that the sentence in (16) cannot be derived from (17a) and (17b) without changing its meaning.

(16) o　　so　　fun　　mi.

　　　　he　　said　　give　　me

　　　　'He told me. '　　　　　　　　　　　(*Bamgbose* 1974 : 31)

(17) *a.* o　　so.

　　　　　he　　said

　　　　　'he said. '　　　　　　　　　　　(*Bamgbose* 1974 : 31)

　　　 b. o　　fun　　mi.

　　　　　he　　gave　　me

　　　　　'He gave me. '　　　　　　　　　　(*Bamgbose* 1974 : 31)

In the sentence (16) , *the semantics of* fun *' give' is bleached and it functions to indicate a kind of grammatical relation like a dative case marker. Similar effects of grammatical category change have also been observed in Mandarin. Certain verbs such as* gei *' give; dative marker' and* ba *' take hold of; object marker' are susceptible to category changes, too. In later chapters of this monograph, we will see similar effects of category change (grammaticalization) and re-lexicalization in Mandarin multi-verb sequences.*

Bamgbose's treatment of SVCs is within the framework of Chomsky's early transformational grammar (1957, 1965). Although Chomsky does not discuss the serial verb phenomena per se in his early transformational grammar books (Syntactic Structures *and* Aspects for the Theory of

Syntax) , the transformational apparatus is often employed to generate SVCs from underlying structures.

2.1.5 Baker (1989)

Baker (1989) proposes a Generalized Serialization Parameter from the perspective of Government and Binding Theory to capture differences among languages which have or lack SVCs. He takes a narrow view of SVCs and treats them as a purely syntactic phenomenon involving nothing more than two verbs in the same clause which share an object and, thus, assign the same theta marking to it as in (18b).

(18) *a.* Aje   gbe   aso   wo.

         Aje   *took*   *dress*   *wear*

         '*Aje took dress (to) wear.* '   (*Baker* 1989 : 516)

b.

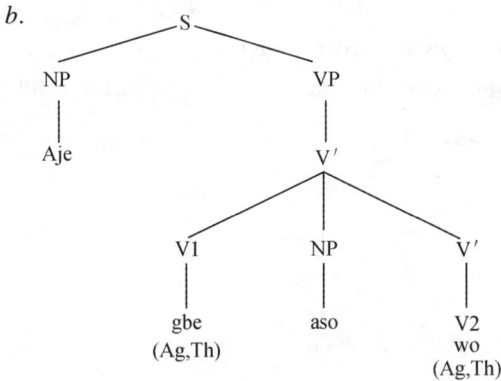

It can be seen from the structure in (18b) that the theta-marking of the NP aso by the V1 is straight-forward, but how V2 can also theta-mark the same NP does not seem to be obvious. In order to account for this, Baker relies on the standard conditions of theta-role assignment, which are stated as follows (1989 : 520) :

α may theta-mark β iff:

    (a) α and β are structural sisters;

    (b) a projection of α is a structural sister of β.

Condition（a）accounts for the theta-marking of the NP by V1 while condition（b）permits the theta-marking of the NP by V2, whose projection is a structural sister to the NP. Baker claims that both verbs are heads and both project to the higher level. VP and V′ are projections of both V1 and V2. As shown in this Yoruba sentence, Baker（1989）claims that the two verbs *gbe* 'took' and *wo* 'wear' share the same direct object and so assign the same theta marking to *aso* 'dress'. He argues that object-sharing by two verbs is the crucial feature of real SVCs.

The sentence in（18）involves two transitive verbs which share an object. Baker argues that his framework can also account for cases which contain a triadic verb（that is, a three-place predicate）as shown in the Ewe sentence in（19）.

（19）a. *O   ra   isu   fun   mi.*
　　　　　he   buy   yam   give   me
　　　　　'He bought a yam for me.'　　　　　　（Baker 1989: 514）

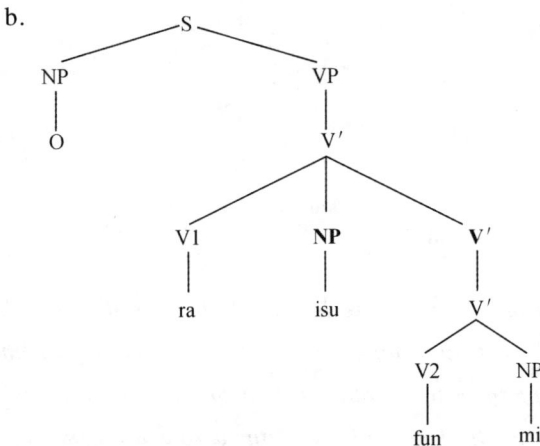

b.
```
                    S
          ┌─────────┴─────────┐
          NP                   VP
          │                    │
          O                    V′
                       ┌───────┼───────┐
                       V1      NP       V′
                       │       │        │
                       ra      isu      V′
                                    ┌───┴───┐
                                    V2      NP
                                    │       │
                                    fun     mi
```

Baker believes that sentence（19a）is a kind of SVC since *ra* 'buy' and *fun* 'give' share the same object *isu* 'yam'. The phenomenon of the theta-marking of the NP by both verbs can be accounted for by expanding the last V′ into a V and NP as in（19b）. In this case, according to

Baker, V2 is able to theta-mark the NP between V1 and V2 since the projection of V2 *fun* 'give' is V', which is a structural sister to the NP *isu* 'yam'.

Baker's SVC definition is based exclusively on the Shared Object Criterion and ignores any other criteria such as semantic interdependence between the two verbs. As such, his definition applies to limited types of SVCs and rules out other constructions that are called SVCs by others.

2.1.6 Agbedor (1994)

Agbedor (1994) claims that Baker's SVC model (1989) mainly accounts for cases involving transitive verbs in which the V1 only takes one argument. If the V1 in an SVC that takes an extra argument, his model is no longer workable, as shown in the Ewe example in (20):

(20a) *Kofi   ɖe   awua   le   ka   dzi   da   ɖe   xō   me.*

      Kofi   remove   shirt   on   rope   top   put   LOC   room   in

      'Kofi removed the shirt from the line and put it in the room. '

(Agbedor 1994: 123)

(20b)

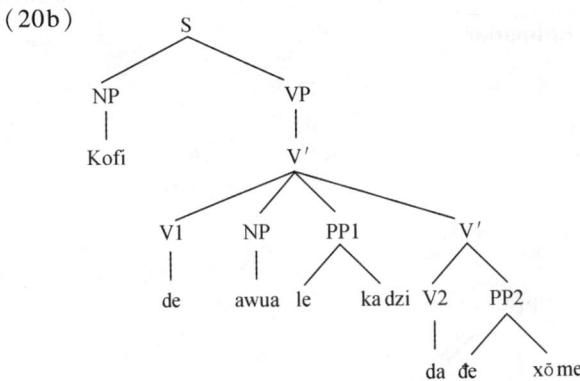

In (20a), the V1 assigns an additional theta role to the PP1. If Baker's model is used to apply to the sentence in (20a), it would be expected that the V2 would theta-mark the PP argument of the V1, PP1. As shown in (20b), the projection of V2 is a sister to both the NP and the PP1.

According to Baker, the sharing of the NP by the two verbs is obligatory and the two verbs should theta-mark the NP between them. In addition, since the PP1 is an argument of V1 as well and a sister to the projection of V2, it would be expected that V2 should also theta-mark PP1. However, this is not the case. This poses a violation of the Projection Principle and the standard conditions on theta marking proposed by Baker.

Agbedor also points out that there are other cases which Baker's model fails to account for. He provides the following Ewe sentence as an example.

(21) *Kofi   no   tsi   ku.*
     Kofi   drink   water   die
     ' Kofi died by drinking water. '　　　(Agbedor 1994 : 123)

In the above sentence, *ku* ' die ' is an intransitive verb, and thus, Baker's object-sharing does not apply here. To account for this example, Baker claims that if two verbs theta-mark the same NP intervening between them, the structure (22a) is projected. However, if only the first verb theta-marks the intervening NP, the structure in (22b) which Baker calls "covert co-ordination" is projected.

(22) (a)　　　　　　　　　　　　(b)

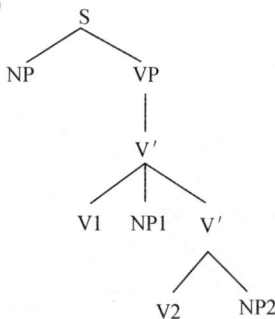 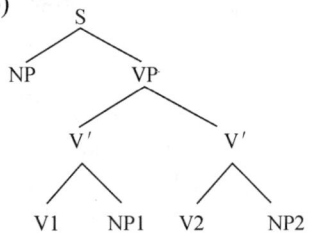

(Agbedor 1994:124)

Baker proposes that the Projection Principle enables V2 to theta-mark NP1 in (19a), but this condition does not exist for (22b). He claims that NP1 is not theta-marked by V2 in the structure of (22b) since the

NP is not sister to V2 or any of its projection. Baker views the structure in (22b) as a case of "covert co-ordination", which denotes a sequence of distinct events, whereas a true SVC signals a single event. What Baker suggests here is that cases of "covert co-ordination" are not true SVCs. Agbedor maintains that this position is not acceptable as it is hard to maintain that the sentence in (21) is a co-ordinate structure which indicates two distinct events. Agbedor claims that sentences like (21) are also true SVCs.

According to Agbedor, one other problem for Baker's model is the case where the two VPs do not share an object as in (23).

(23) *Kofi   tutu   devia   dze   anyi.*

Kofi   push   the. child   fall   down

' Kofi pushed the child and fell down. '

(Agbedor 1994: 124)

In this Ewe sentence in (23), V2 can not theta-mark the NP of V1 since the sentence only has one interpretation, that is, Kofi pushes the child and Kofi fell down. Therefore, there is no object-sharing in this sentence and Baker's model fails to account for this true SVC in Ewe.

Agbedor has shown that the Ewe language poses certain problems for Baker's model, especially regarding the Projection Principle and the concept of object-sharing. He suggests that Baker's classification of the true and non-true SVC should be rejected. In order to improve upon Baker's model, Agbedor presents an alternative analysis to handle the Ewe SVC data. He proposes a structure for SVCs in which a double-headed VP splits into two V single bars. He follows Baker (1989) in having double-headed VPs but he differs in the way that VPs are projected in the tree, as shown in (24).

(24)

```
              S
           /     \
         NP       VP
               /      \
             V'        V'
            /  \      /   \
          V1   NP1  V2    NP2
```

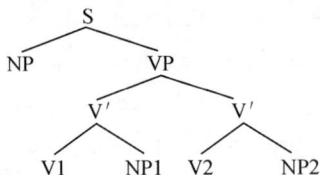

(Agbedor 1994:124)

Agbedor further suggests that a null (empty) object for V2 is expected to be coindexed with the object of V1 in cases of SVCs involving object-sharing. This proposal avoids problems where V2 is unable to theta-mark an additional argument such as a PP, thus violating the Projection Principle proposed by Baker. This suggests that the phenomenon of the object sharing should be dealt with in a different way than Baker suggests. According to Agbedor's analysis, the sentence in (25a) should have the structure in (25b).

(25) a. *Kofi   fo   devia   wu.*

　　　 Kofi   beat   the. child   kill

　　　 'Kofi beat the child to death.'　　　(Agbedor 1994: 128)

b.

```
              S
           /     \
         NP       VP
               /      \
             V'        V'
            /  \      /   \
          V1   NP1  V2    NP2
          |     |    |     |
          fo  devia  wu    e
```

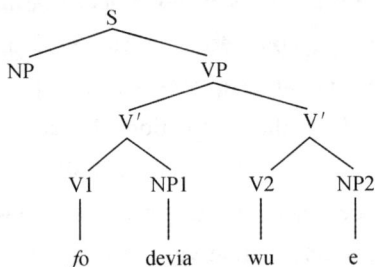

(Agbedor 1994:128)

Agbedor believes that his proposal would avoid at least two problems for Baker's SVC framework. It avoids the inability of V2 to theta-mark a PP argument of V1 since, in Agbedor's proposal, the projection of V2 is no longer the sister of the PP even though this PP position satisfies the condition for theta-marking under Baker's proposal. In addition, his proposal accounts for non-sharing of an NP between V1 and V2 in some SVCs. He claims that V2 does not have to share an NP object with V1 unless V2 has a null object coindexed with the object of V1. Although his proposal is able to avoid some of the problems of Baker's analysis, Agbedor is aware that the notion of an empty object in SVCs is quite theory-specific at best and ad hoc at worst and needs to be further researched. Moreover, his proposal has to be tested with other SVC languages to establish its universality. Agbedor also realizes that there are still more questions than answers despite the extensive and intensive research on SVCs in the past dozens of years and that even the issue of what constitutes a real SVC is not clear.

2.1.7 *Aikhenvald* (2006)

A recent book, *Serial Verb Constructions: A Cross-linguistic Typology* (Aikhenvald & Dixon 2006), attempts to shed some cross-linguistic light on SVCs. This study acknowledges that certain languages from West Africa, East Asia, and Oceania are well known for their serial verb constructions and it provides a framework which covers the major cross-linguistic parameters for serial verbs. In the introduction, Aikhenvald defines an SVC as a sequence of verbs which act as a single predicate, without any overt marker of coordination, subordination or any other syntactic dependency. She claims that an SVC denotes a single event conceptually. "They are monoclausal; their international properties are the same as those of a monoverbal clause, and they have just one tense, aspect, and polarity" (Aikhenvald, 2006: 1). She presents an overview of SVCs which covers cross-linguistically attested parameters of variation and formulates generalizations regarding different types of SVCs. Aikhenvald claims that SVCs can be classified on the basis of four parameters: composition, contiguity, wordhood of the components, and grammatical inflection of elements within the SVC.

In terms of composition, SVCs can be classified as a symmetrical type and an asymmetrical type. Symmetrical SVCs contain two verbs, each of which comes from a semantically and grammatically unrestricted class. An example is given in (26):

Alamblak (Aikhenvald 2006: 11)

(26) *mɨyt*   *ritm*   *muh-hambray-an-m*

     tree   insects   climb-search-1SG-3PL

     'I climbed the tree searching for insects. '

As in (26), each verb in symmetrical SVCs comes from unrestricted classes and the order of the component verbs are more likely to be iconic, reflecting the temporal sequence of its sub-events. This kind of SVC is not headed since its component verbs have equal status and none of them acts as a head or determines the semantic or syntactic properties of the whole construction.

On the contrary, an asymmetrical SVC contains a verb from a semantically or grammatically restricted class. This kind of SVC expresses a single conceptual event described by the main verb from a non-restricted class. The verb from the closed class serves as modification. It is often the case that motion or posture verbs signal direction or provide a tense or aspectual meaning to the construction as a whole. An example from Cantonese is given in (27)

Cantonese (Matthews 2006: 76)

(27) *lei*   *lo*   *di*   *saam*   *lai*

     you   take   PL   clothing   come

     'Bring some clothes. '

In (27), the verb *lai* 'come' provides directional specification to the SVC and *lo...lai* here together mean 'bring'. Aikhenvald claims that the transitivity value of asymmetrical SVCs is normally the same as that of the verb from the open class, and thus, this verb acts as the 'head' of the construction both syntactically and semantically. The verb from the unrestricted class is considered the 'major' verb while the verb from a grammatically restricted class is termed the 'minor' verb. Minor verbs in asymmetrical SVCs often get or have been grammaticalized.

SVCs can also be classified into two types: contiguous and non-contiguous. Verbs in contiguous SVCs usually have to be next to each other while verbs in non-contiguous SVCs may allow another constituent to intervene. Consider the examples in (28) and (29):

Alamblak (Aikhenvald 2006: 2)

(28) wa-yarim-ak-hɨta-n-m-ko

　　　IMP-ELEV-GET-PUT-2SG-3PL-ELEV

　　　'Get them on a level plane toward me (and) put them up there.'

Cantonese (Mathews 2006: 74)

(29) ngo   bong   lei   daa   din-waa

　　　I   help   you   make   phone-call

　　　'I'll make a phone call for you.'

In (28), an instance of a contiguous SVC, the two component verbs ak hɨta 'get put' do not allow other constituents to go between them. However, as a non-contiguous SVC, (29) does allow another constituent lei 'you' to intervene between its two component verbs bong 'help' and daa 'make'.

The third parameter used to classify SVCs is wordhood of the components: verb components in an SVC may or may not constitute independent lexical words. Therefore, by the wordhood criterion, SVCs can be grouped into one-word or multi-word constructions. Verb components in some SVCs may function as independent lexical words; that is, each verb could act as a well-formed predicate in its own right as in (30). Alternatively, the component verbs in an SVC can function as one complex lexical word and the verbs in this kind of SVC are often referred to as 'compounding' or 'Root Serialization', as in (31).

Baule (Kwa, Niger-Congo: Aikhenvald 2006: 2)

(30) ɔ-à-fà   í   swǎ   n   à-klè   mɪ

　　　he-ANT-take   his   house   DEF   ANT-show   me

　　　'He has shown me his house' (take-show)

Alamblak (Aikhenvald 2006: 11)

(31) mɨyt   guñm   muh-hɨti-marña-an-m

tree   stars   climb-see-well-1SG-3PL

'I climbed the tree seeing the stars clearly'

Inflectional marking of verbal components in an SVC is another parameter proposed to classify SVCs. Typically, verb inflection includes categories such as "person of the subject and object; tense, aspect, modality, mood, evidentiality; valence changing; word class changing derivations; illocutionary force; and discourse categories such as focus" (Aikhenvald 2006: 39). Within an SVC, each of these categories could be marked on every verb component and this kind of marking is called concordant marking. Alternatively, a grammatical category can be marked once per construction, which is referred to as single marking. These marking alternatives are shown in (32) and (33), respectively.

Akan (Aikhenvald 2006: 40)

(32) *mede*   *aburow*   *migu*   *msulm*

1SG. take   corn   1SG. flow   water. in

'I pour corn into water'

Paamese (Aikhenvald 2006: 42)

(33) *samsene* *mungali*   *vaasi* *velaase-nV*   *laisne*

Sampson   3SG + REALIS + rip. open   split   jaw-CONSTRUCT. STATE   lion

'Sampson split apart the lion's jaw'

In (32), the person of the subject (first person singular) is marked on both verbs *mede* 'take' and *migu* 'flow'. In (33), the subject marker only occurs once and the person of the subject (third person singular) is only marked on the first verb, not the second.

Aikhenvald (2006) presents parameters of cross-linguistical variation and formulates generalizations regarding the types of SVCs observed and the properties associated with them. However, she claims that in a particular language SVCs are expected to have some or most, but not necessarily all of the relevant properties. She suggests a scalar approach to serial verb constructions. She believes that SVCs cover a wide range of meanings and functions and are not a single grammatical category. They display semantic and functional similarities to multi-clausal and subordinating constructions in non-serial verb languages. These similarities indicate that SVCs are part of a multi-dimensional continuum of multi-verb structures and SVCs have become a focal point within a continuum of multi-verb constructions (Aikhenvald 2006). Aikhenvald recognizes that " despite the considerable literature on verb serialization much remains to be investigated in order to obtain a further cross-linguistic perspective on its varied facets" (2006 : 57).

2.2 *Past Approaches to Chinese SVCs*

Like analyses of SVCs in other languages, those of Mandarin SVCs are greatly varied. Definitions of SVCs range from the very broad, which includes almost all sequences which contain two verbs as SVCs, to the very narrow, which subsumes only one type of SVC such as the object-sharing case of Baker (1989).

2.2.1 *Chao* (1968)

Chao (1968) proposes that SVCs in Mandarin Chinese form an intermediate type between coordinate and subordinate constructions, but are nearer to the latter than the former. A V-V sequence that's a true SVC is like a coordinate phrase in that both parts are verbal expressions, usually with an object after the first verb. However, Chao maintains that a coordinate verbal expression is reversible without affecting the value of the sentence, but a V-V sequence, when reversed, often has a different semantic value.

In a coordinate construction as in (31a), the V-V sequence can be reversed (31b) without changing the meaning.

(34) a. *Ta   jingchang   tiaowu   change.*

      3SG   often   dance   sing

      ' S/he often dances and sings. '

    b. *Ta*   *jingchang*   *change*   *tiaowu.*

    3SG   often   sing   dance

    'S/he often sings and dances. '

However, in a true SVC as in (35a), the reversal of the two verbs can and does change the interpretation, as (35b) shows.

(35) a. *Qu*   *deng*   *yihuier.*

       go   wait   a while

      'Go (and) wait a while. '   (Chao 1968: 326)

    b. *Deng*   *yihuier*   *qu.*

       wait   a while   go

      'Wait a while (before you) go. '   (Chao 1968: 326)

It is true that SVCs are different from typical coordinate constructions, as Chao claims. However, according to him, a V-V series is like a subordinate construction in that the second verb serves as the main verb of the construction, and thus, it is the head to which the first verbal expression is a modifier, often translatable by a prepositional or other modifying phrase. As such, by his definition, most of his SVC sentences involve coverbs as in (36). In this example, the coverb *cong* 'from' is no longer a lexical verb and its source meaning 'follow' as a verb has been completely bleached. As a coverb, it does not suggest any aspectualized event but simply indicates location (source of motion).

(36) *Ta*   *cong*   *Zhongguo*   *lai.*

    3SG   from   China   come

    'S/he came from China. '

Even typical case markers in Mandarin Chinese like *ba* (object marker) and *bei* (passive marker) as in (37) and (38) are included in his taxonomy of serial verb constructions.

(37) *Ta*   *ba*   *ge*   *pibao*   *diu*   *le.*

    3SG   BA   CL   wallet   lose   PERF

    'S/he lost the wallet. '(Chao 1968: 344)

(38) *Wo*   *bei*   *ta*   *pian*   *le.*

I   BEI   3SG   fool   PERF

'I was fooled by him/her. '   (Chao 1968: 330)

The original verb meaning *ba* 'take hold of' or *bei* 'cover, receive' is no longer present in (37) and (38). These two coverbs profile participants rather than actions. Now, most modern Chinese linguists think that typical coverbs act differently to a large extent than lexical verbs. In fact, most of the instances in Chao's SVC category are not typical SVCs but rather coverb constructions.

2.2.2 Li and Thompson (1981)

Li and Thompson (1981) define Mandarin serial verbs as "two or more verb phrases or clauses juxtaposed together without any marker indicating what relationship is between them (594). " According to Li and Thompson (ibid. : 595), Chinese serial verbs may be categorized as follows:

i. Two or more separate events (alternating, consecutive, circumstance and purpose)

ii. One verb phrase/clause serving as subject or direct object of another

iii. Pivotal constructions, in which one NP serves as both the object of VP1 and the logical subject of VP2

iv. Descriptive clauses

Li and Thompson's classification (1981) includes constructions with two or more clauses and largely discounts the nature of the interdependence between them. Consequently, their classification of Mandarin SVCs is rather broad and encompasses structures such as coordinate clauses as in (39), in which the two VPs do not bear any temporal or other interdependent relation.

(39) *Ta   tian   tian   chang   ge   xie   xin.*

    3SG   day   day   sing   song   write   letter

    'S/he sings songs and writes letters every day. '

(Li & Thompson 1981: 595)

Their classification also covers typical complement clauses under their sub-type (ii) as in (40).

(40) Ta   fouren   ta   zuo   cuo   le.

  3SG   deny   3SG   do   wrong   PERF

  ' S/he confessed that (s/he) had done something wrong. '

(Li & Thompson 1981: 598)

Even relative clause constructions with the overt relative clause marker *de* are included in their SVC categories (under their sub-type (iv): Descriptive clauses) as in (41):

(41) Ta   yang   le   yi   tiao   wo   yao   mai   de   gou.

  3SG   raise   PERF   one   CL   I   want   buy   poss   dog

  ' S/he has raised one of those dogs which I want to buy. '

(Li & Thompson 1981: 615)

Li and Thompson's classification of SVCs aims to be widely inclusive in order to cover major types of multi-verb sequences in Mandarin which they think possess characteristics of SVCs. However, Chang (1990) claims that their classification of SVCs includes all kinds of irrelevant structures as SVCs such as coordination as in (39) and subordination as in (40), but leaves out relevant structures as non-SVCs such as the kind of the multi-verb construction in which both verbs share a subject and an object as well.

2.2.3 Dai (1990)

Different from the previous analyses, Dai's classification of verb serialization only applies to one type of multi-verb construction, that is, the *lai*-construction. He (1990) distinguishes three types of serial verb expressions in Chinese: coordination, subordination and serialization. His so-called verb serialization type is formed by a pair of V1 plus V2 (NP), in which V1 consists of the verb *lai* ' come ' or *qu* ' go ' as the following examples show (cf. Chen 1993: 42):

(42) Ta   lai   shang   ban   le.

3SG   come   ascend   shift   PERF

'S/he came to work. '

(43) *Ta   qu   guang   gongyuan   le.*

3SG   go   wonder   park   PERF.

'S/he went to see a park. '

Dai (1990) believes that there is no constraint on the V2 in a serial verb construction. He calls this kind of verb construction the *lai*-construction (referred to as motion constructions in my analysis below). He claims that this construction, structurally different from either coordinate or subordinate constructions though sharing some properties with them, is a marked construction and the only true SVC in Chinese.

Dai suggests that verb constituents in serialization and coordination both bear the same grammatical relation to the single overt external argument, that is, they share the subject, but there is no grammatical relation between the constituents themselves. The latter morphosyntactic feature distinguishes serialization and coordination from subordination.

Dai states that verb constituents in coordination do not bear any grammatical relation to each other and, thus, are independent from each other. However, verb constituents in subordination hold a dependency relationship between them. According to Dai, the two verb phrases in coordination are sisters and both have main verb status. Therefore, coordinate structures are double-headed. By contrast, the two VPs in subordination are not symmetrical or even at the same level syntactically. Only one of them is the main verb. The one which has the main verb status is the head and, thus, subordinate structures are single-headed.

The distinction between serialization and coordination lies in the difference between single-headedness in the former case and multi-headedness in the latter. The following is an example of a so-called typical SVC provided by Dai.

(44) *Ta   lai   xuexi   yingyu.*

3SG   come   study   English

'S/he came to study English.'　　　　　(Dai 1990: 318)

Dai suggests that *xuexi* 'study' and *yingyu* 'English' do not form a constituent in this sentence since *lai* 'come' and *xuexi* 'study' form a compound. He claims that "one of the crucial properties of the SVC is that no element of any sort may intervene between V1 + V2 in the *lai*-construction" (1990: 318-319). It seems to him that the intervention constraint provides a strong piece of evidence to support the claim that the two verbs in the *lai*-construction form a compound. Dai maintains that, as a compound, V1 and V2 form a constituent with a single head in this kind of construction. However, V1 and V2 in coordination structures are independent and each verb forms its own head. Therefore, the important criterion to distinguish coordination and serialization is whether it is double-headed or single-headed, with the possibility of intervening material being the major diagnostic between them.

Chen (1993) points out that Dai's strong claim that nothing (neither the argument nor modifier of V1 or V2) may intervene between the verbs in serialization such as in the *lai*-construction is not entirely true. It is the case that *lai* in the *lai*-construction does not allow any complements of time. As a result, no temporal phrase may intervene between *lai* and the verb which follows it, as the following example illustrates:

(45) * *Ta*　　*lai*　　*san*　　*xiaoshi*　　*xuexi*　　*yingyu*.

　　　3SG　　come　　three　　hour　　　study　　English

　　　* 'S/he came for three hours to study English.' (Chen 1993: 46)

Chen (1993) suggests that sub-categorization restrictions on *lai* proscribing any complements of time are at work, not that *lai* cannot take any complement in the *lai*-construction. In fact, it is fully legitimate for *lai* to take complements of place, as (46) demonstrates:

(46) *Ta*　　*lai*　　*Yadian*　　*xuexi*　　*yingyu*.

　　　3SG　　come　　Athens　　study　　English

　　　'S/he came to Athens to study English.'　(Chen 1993: 47)

In the *lai*-construction, *lai* not only is subcategorized to take complements of place, but it also allows its own modifiers. It is the same situation with the V2 which can take a complement and/or a modifier in this kind of construction.

(47) *Ta*　　*jingchang*　　*qu*　　*xuexiao*　　*nuli*　　*xuexi yingyu*.

3SG　　often　　　　go　　school　　hard　　study　English.

' S/he often came to school to study English hard. '

(Chen 1993: 47)

In Mandarin Chinese, a modifier precedes its head. An adverbial also usually precedes the verb it modifies. In (47), *jingchang* ' often ' modifies the verb *qu* ' go ' while *nuli* ' hard ' modifies *xuexi* ' study '.

Example (47) shows that both V1 and V2 can take complements and allow modifiers respectively. The complement of *qu* virtually acts as the intervening element between V1 and V2. Dai's claim that no element can intervene between V1 and V2 in the *lai*-construction simply does not hold and, thus, V1 and V2 in this kind of construction do not really form a compound. The fact is that most of the cases in motion constructions which involve *lai/qu* as V1 do not take overt complements. My evidence comes from the corpus data (the Lancaster Corpus of Mandarin Chinese with one million written words), which will be discussed in detail in later chapters. The higher probability for *lai/qu* not to take any covert complements does not warrant the conclusion that *lai/qu* does not take any complement at all in SVCs. Actually, the kind of *lai*-construction in which *lai/qu* does not take any intervening complement between V1 and V2 suggests a more conflated event integration and a tighter purposive construction than otherwise. Dai's *lai*-construction is only one kind of SVC and perhaps the canonical SVC; however, it is not the only type of SVC, as Dai claims it to be.

2.2.4 *Paul* (2004)

More recently, Paul (2004) points out that the term " serial verb construction" as currently used in Chinese linguistics simply refers to any surface string with more than one verb. It subsumes a multitude of different structures. He thinks that the term SVC is often used when in need of a *passepartout* label for a badly understood structure in Chinese. He takes Li and Thompson's view of SVC as representative of the current practice in the field since their work has been quite influential in Chinese linguistics. After having carefully examined Li and Thompson's SVC types (1981) one by one, he argues that in Chinese linguistics "SVC" has served as a cover term for distinct constructions with different properties. According to Li and Thompson, the term serial verb construction refers to a sentence that contains two or more verb phrases or clauses juxtaposed without any marker indicating what the relationship is between them. Paul identifies at least seven types of SVCs in Li and Thompson's classification. He believes that their SVC type denoting two or more separate events is a kind of coordinate construction while the SVC type in which one verb phrase or clause is the subject or direct object of another verb is certainly a kind of subordinate construction. Thus, he argues that different constructions are involved here, with a different set of syntactic and semantic properties in each case. According to Paul, to call all of them "SVCs" amounts to no more than stating that they all contain two (or more) verbs. According to Paul, the term SVC in Mandarin Chinese, despite its claim to the status of construction, is nothing but a surface label for denoting the linear sequence of constituents and in no case gives us any indication as to the syntactic structure of the sequence at hand.

According to Paul, since "Chinese SVC" in Chinese linguistics has served as a cover term for distinct constructions with different properties and it does not refer to a unique construction with a predictable set of properties, the term SVC in its current use in Chinese linguistics is shown to be too vague to be of any use. Therefore, he proposes to abandon it altogether and suggests making a fresh start. In order to make the SVC a unique construction he adopts a narrow definition of SVC as object-sharing in the sense of Collins (1997) and believes that the so-called directional verb compounds as shown in (48) and (49) are real SVCs in Chinese. Such compounds refer to verb sequences of the type 'Vdisplacement (-Vdirection) -come/go' such as *song lai* 'send come - send over', which he believes have so far not received a satisfactory analysis. In this type of verb sequence, the first constituent is a displacement verb, the second one is a direction verb which is optional, and the last one is the motion verb *lai* 'come' or *qu* 'go'.

(48) a. *Ta* *song-le* *yi-ge* *xiangzi* *lai*.

  3SG send-PERF one-CL suitcase come

  ' S/he sent a suitcase over here. ' (Paul 2004: 17)

 b. *Ta* *song-lai-le* *yi-ge* *xiangzi*.

  3SG send-come-PERF one-CL suitcase

  ' S/he sent a suitcase over here. ' (Paul 2004: 17)

(49) a. *Ta* *duan-le* *yi-wan* *tang* *shang-lai* *le*.

  3SG serve-PERF one-bowl soup ascend-come PART

  ' S/he served up a bowl of soup (towards the speaker). '

            (Paul 2004: 18)

 b. *Ta* *duan-shang-lai-le*   *yi-wan* *tang* le.

  3SG serve-ascend-come-PERF one-bowl soup part

  ' S/he served up a bowl of soup (towards the speaker). '

            (Paul 2004: 18)

Paul argues that the strings of the form ' Vdisplacement (-Vdirection) - come/go' cannot be compounds since the first verb can be suffixed with the perfective aspect marker *-le* and the object can occupy a position within the sequence, as (48a) and (49a) show. He thinks such strings should be excluded from verbal compounds such as *pi-ping*, ' criticize-judge - criticize ', *pao-qi* ' throw-discard - abandon ', *chi-wan* ' eat-finish - eat up ', given the *Lexical Integrity Hypothesis* (cf. Huang 1984), which states that word-internal structure is invisible to syntactic processes. For example, due to the *Lexical Integrity Hypothesis* no other element such as the aspect marker *le* can intervene between the constituents of a lexical compound, as (50a) and (50b) demonstrate.

(50) a. *Ta   pi-ping-le*   *Akiu.*

    3SG   criticize-judge-PERF   Akiu.

    ' S/he criticized/abandoned Akiu. '   (Paul 2004: 18)

   b. ** Ta   pi-le-ping*   *Akiu.*

     3SG   criticize-PERF-judge   Akiu (Paul 2004: 18)

   c. ** Ta   pi(-le)*   *Akiu   ping.*

    3SG   criticize-PERF   Akiu   judge (Paul 2004: 18)

(51) a. *Ta   chi-wan-le*   *wanfan.*

    3SG   eat-finish-PERF   dinner

    ' S/he ate up his dinner. '   (Paul 2004: 18)

   b. ** Ta   chi-le-wan*   *wanfan.*

     3SG   eat-PERF-finish   dinner

             (Paul 2004: 18)

   c. ** Ta   chi(-le)*   *wanfan   wan.*

    3SG   eat-PERF   dinner   finish

             (Paul 2004: 18)

Paul suggests that the clear contrast between the verbal compounds in (50)-(51) and the sequences ' Vdisplacement(-Vdirection)-come/go ' in (48)-(49) in terms of the object position and the placement of the aspect marker *le* challenges the alleged compound status of the latter since the two verbs in either (50) or (51) do allow *le* or an object to intervene between them. He argues that the data given above show that ' Vdisplacement(-Vdirection)-come/go ' strings do not behave on a par with verbal compounds and must therefore be analysed as phrases. He believes that to assign such verb sequences the structure of an internal argument-sharing SVC allows us to better account for their syntactic and semantic properties: the object of the first verb is also the internal argument of the verb *lai/qu* or its combination with a directional verb.

    Paul acknowledges that more research needs to be done to flesh out the analysis of the so-called "directional verb compounds" with regard to an internal argument-sharing SVC. However, he claims that even at this preliminary stage, a positive result has been obtained from having discarded the old term SVC with its numerous definitions and that by doing this it allows us to make a fresh start and to give new and exact content to the term SVC. He believes that the application of the narrow definition of SVC as an internal argument-sharing construction sheds new light on the analysis of this so far rather poorly understood phenomenon. It seems that Paul was right in discarding the old term SVC and reexamining the phenomenon of verb serialization.

2.3 Discussion

From the above discussion about past treatments of SVCs, it is apparent that there is little consensus for either what is or is not an SVC or for sub-classifications within the SVC category as a whole. For lack of agreed-upon criteria, different linguists have given different classifications to these structurally similar multi-verb constructions in Chinese. Chinese morphosyntax is so impoverished or underspecified, which largely explains why everyone comes up with a different set of what is in or out of the serial verb construction category. The aim of this study is to address different kinds of constructions which consist of more than one verb and provide an integrated and unified account for what is and what is not an SVC in Mandarin Chinese. By proposing that multi-verb sequences are of a graded phenomenon and display degrees of event integration, my analysis can account for all types of serial verb sequences in Mandarin Chinese. I will argue that degree of event integration in multi-verb constructions is the key idea, an idea that takes its inspiration from Cognitive Grammar. In the next chapter, I will discuss some basic tenets of this framework.

Chapter Three

Basic Tenets of Cognitive Grammar

Since my analysis of Mandarin Chinese multi-verb sequences is based on Cognitive Grammar (Langacker 1987, 1990, 1991, 1999), it will be helpful to introduce some of its main tenets. In this section, I will discuss the basic assumptions and concepts of this framework.

3.1 *Assumptions of Cognitive Grammar*

Cognitive Grammar (CG) assumes that language structure is the product of our interaction with the world around us. The way we develop linguistic categories can be derived from the way we experience our environment and use that experience for communication (Langacker 1987). Langacker (1987) believes that we are less worried about what kind of syntax or phonology to use than we are about how to encode meanings we want to communicate. Language use is goal-oriented in the way that people use language to accomplish purposes and goals. Langacker (1987) argues that linguistic forms tend to adapt to meanings expressed by them and not normally the other way around. Therefore, it is reasonable to assume that the structural organization of language is meaning-driven rather than form-driven.

CG emerges organically from a comprehensive and unified view of linguistic organization characterized in terms of cognitive processing (Langacker 1987). CG views language as an integral part of human cognition. Langacker (1987) claims that no matter whether one posits an innate faculty or a special language "module", an account of linguistic structure should articulate what is known about general cognitive processing. He argues that if such a faculty does exist, it should be embedded in a general cognitive matrix, since it represents the evolution and fixation of structures with a less specialized origin. We do not have valid reasons to expect a sharp dichotomy between linguistic ability and other aspects of cognition. Instead of trying to grasp at any apparent rationale for asserting the uniqueness of language, we should make efforts to integrate the findings of linguistics and cognition (Langacker 1987).

Langacker (1987) claims that linguistic structure is a direct reflection of cognition in the way that a particular linguistic expression is associated with a particular way of conceptualization. It would be better for us to understand language structure with reference to its conceptual foundations. Langacker (1987) argues that some linguistic forms are meaningless if we take them literally, but they can be accounted for if reference is given to the cognitive factors which are responsible for their growth. Thus, our primary concern should be the underlying concepts which are responsible for selecting a particular form or meaning (Langacker 1987). Language structures reflect patterns of human conceptualization because they are shaped by such patterns.

CG (Langacker 1991) assumes that grammar and meaning are indissociable and that meaning is a cognitive phenomenon. CG therefore identifies meaning with our conceptualization, that is, with our mental experience (Langacker 1991: 4). Langacker (1987, 1991) believes that semantic structure should be considered to be encyclopaedic in scope and that the meaning of a linguistic unit involves specifications in many cognitive domains. Some of the cognitive domains involved are more central to its value than others. Semantic units are relative to cognitive domains and any concept or knowledge system can function as a cognitive domain (Langacker 1987).

One of the focal concerns of CG involves semantic structure, which is based on conventional imagery. "Our capacity to construe the same content in different ways is referred to as imagery; expressions describing the same conceived situation may nonetheless be semantically quite distinct by virtue of the contrasting images they impose on it" (Langacker 1991: 4). In fact, grammar embodies imagery. It structures a situation in a particular way, viewing it from a certain perspective, stressing certain facets of the situation at the expense of others, or construing it in terms of metaphor or metonymy (Langacker 1987).

CG maintains that lexicon and grammar form a continuum. Only symbolic structures - each residing in the symbolic linkage of a semantic and a phonological structure figure in their proper characterization of a linguistic expression (Langacker 1987, 1991). In the case of the wide range of constructions that are associated with Mandarin multi-verb sequences, these constructions form a continuum between lexicon and grammar as well. In the range of multi-verb constructions, some are more fixed and more lexical and some are more open and more productive. The key idea is that they form a cline of integration just as they form a cline of fixedness.

3.2 Symbolization

CG is driven by the assumption that language is essentially and inherently symbolic in nature (Langacker 1987, 1988, 1991, 1999). Langacker (1987, 1991) proposes that grammar can essentially reduce to the structuring and symbolization of conceptual content and it has no autonomous existence at all. CG "ascribes to language an organization that is both natural and minimal granted its communicative function of allowing conceptualizations to be symbolized by phonological sequences" (Langacker 1991: 1-2). Thus, Langacker (1987, 1991) claims that any linguistic expression, whether a morpheme, a single word, a phrase or a sentence is comprised of just three components - semantic structures, phonological structures, and the symbolic links between them, as shown in Figure 3. 1.

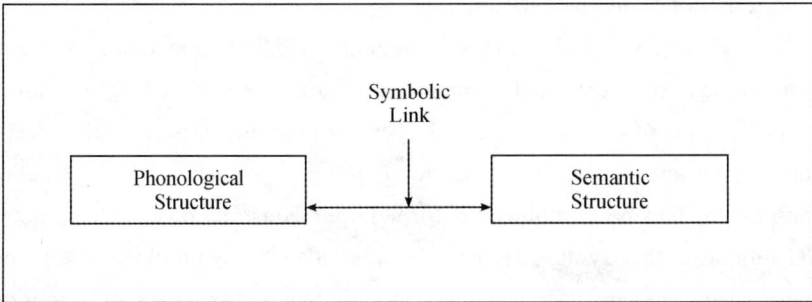

Symbolic
Link

Phonological
Structure

Semantic
Structure

Figure 3. 1   The three components of a linguistic expression, as proposed in CG

Figure 3. 1 shows the organization of any linguistic expression in which only three kinds of components are depicted. CG makes the very strong claim that language can be exhaustively described in terms of these three kinds of components:

(i) Phonological structure refers to the overt manifestation of language, that is, a linguistic expression in its material or perceptible aspects. Typically, a linguistic expression is manifested in the medium of sound, but this component would encompass sign and orthographic representation as well.

(ii) Semantic structure refers to the meaning of an expression. CG views semantic structures as comprising both the propositional content of an expression and the broader conceptualization that language users entertain. Such conceptualization includes perspective, construal, figure-ground alignment and so on. Semantic structure includes pragmatic aspects of meaning as well and it is broadly encyclopaedia in scope.

(iii) Symbolic links hold between phonological poles (structures) and semantic poles. In Figure 2. 1, the arrow linking these two poles points in both directions and this suggests that the link between meaning and sound is a two-way relationship in that each pole of the symbolic relation invokes the other. In CG, symbolic links play an important role and linguistic expressions are largely analysed in terms of symbolic relations.

As Figure 3.1 indicates, CG assumes a direct association between phonological structures and semantic structures. By excluding a distinct syntactic level of organization, CG does not deny the existence of syntax. One important aspect for CG to handle is to show how smaller components can be combined to form larger constructions. What makes CG unique is that syntax itself is considered to be symbolic in the same way that the lexicon is and syntax, too, is handled in terms of symbolic relations between phonological structures and semantic structures (Langacker 1987). Next, I would like to look at how simpler symbolic structures are combined to form larger constructions in CG.

3.3 *Construction and Composition*

CG claims that grammar resides in patterns of expression that combine simpler symbolic units into progressively more complex ones. "Any such combination is referred to as a construction. It consists of two or more component structures that are integrated to from a composite structure. A construction is characterized as an assembly of symbolic structures linked by correspondences and categorizing relationships" (Langacker 1991: 5). Generally, CG does not view component structures as "building blocks" that are stacked together to form the composite structure. Langacker claims that the composite expression often displays emergent properties which are not discernable in any individual component, and that the composite structure can impose an alternate image to that of the component structures (1991: 5). Thus, "the component structures are best described, not as constituting the composite structure, but rather as categorizing certain facets of it and as motivating to some degree the form-meaning pairing that the composite structure embodies" (Langacker 1991 : 6) .

A grammatical construction is a symbolic structure which involves the syntagmatic combination of component structures. Langacker (1987) claims that such a construction consists of component structures, the mode of integration, and the composite structure which results from the integration. Therefore, composition is essential in forming larger constructions. Langacker (1987) refers to the relation between component structures and the composite structures deriving from them as composition. Compositionality concerns such questions as " [i] s the integration of component structures to form a composite structure sufficiently regular to be susceptible to schematic characterization or is it possible to formulate a schema for a particular construction that will enable one to predict, for every potential choice of component structures, precisely what the composite structure will be (Langacker 1987 : 448) ?"

The classical view attributes full semantic compositionality to grammatical constructions. The assumption of compositionality is considered to be necessary to account for the fact that language users are able to produce and understand novel expressions. However, Langacker (1987, 1991) claims that patterns of compositionality are considered to be represented in the grammar as schematic constructions to specify the integration of component parts and the relation between component structures and the composite structure. Langacker argues (1987) that the existence of compositionality patterns does not substantiate the claim that composite structures are fully compositional and that linguistic phenomena are more likely to show partial rather than fully compositionality. There are instances where composite structures evoke knowledge systems to which their components do not provide direct access and in many cases the component structures motivate and highlight certain facets of the composite meaning instead of exhausting its content (Langacker 1987 : 453).

3.4 *Base vs. Profile*

The notion of base/profile is one of the essential concepts in Cognitive Grammar. Langacker (1988) proposes that a semantic structure derives its value through the imposition of a profile on a base. The profile comprises those portions of the base which the entity designates. "Some facet of the base is invariably raised to a distinctive level of prominence, and serves as its focal point; this substructure is the predication's profile" (Langacker 1988: 59). For example, the conception of a right triangle serves as the base for hypotenuse and its profile is one of the line segments, as illustrated in Figure 3.2:

(a) HYPOTENUSE   (b)   (c)

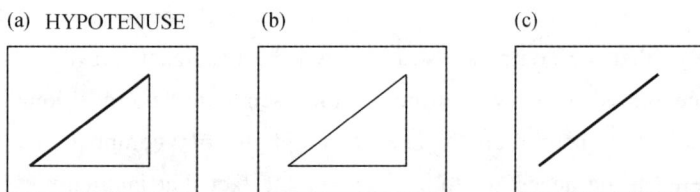

Figure 3.2   Distinction between the base and the profile (Langacker 1988: 59)

In Figure 3.2, the profiled element is represented by the heavy line to indicate the prominence, which distinguishes it from the remainder of the base. Langacker (1988) suggests that an expression's meaning does not lie in either the profile or the base alone and that both of them are important to its value. Profiling involves the elevation of some part of the base to a special level of prominence. If the profiling of *hypotenuse* is suppressed, as in Figure 3.2 (b), what we get is not the conception of hypotenuse, but simply that of a right triangle. However, if the unprofiled portions of the base are suppressed, as in (c), there is no base for identifying the remaining line segment as being a hypotenuse (Langacker 1988), only a diagonal line. Therefore, the base is essential in realizing an expression's meaning by providing the context or the frame to identify the profiled entity or the intended designatum.

3.5 *Construal*

It has been commonly assumed that the role of language is to map elements of the external world onto linguistic form. According to the traditional view, situations can be dissected into component parts, each of which corresponds to certain element of language. Thus, the mapping from the external world to linguistic expression is considered relatively straightforward and this mapping basically involves a one-to-one encoding of the elements of the situation into linguistic structure.

However, CG argues that there is no such direct one-to-one mapping. CG holds that a given situation can be construed in different ways and different ways of construing the same situation represents different conceptualizations. The meaning of the linguistic expression is not just the conceptual content it evokes, but it also depends on the construal it imposes on that content (Langacker 1990). One dimension of construal is the degree of specificity and detail which a language user chooses to conceive and portray a given entity or situation. For example, the decision to describe something as *thing*, *living thing*, *plant*, *tree*, *apple tree* is a matter of construal. Each expression in this series is schematic for the one that follows, which instantiates or elaborates it by providing a finer-grained characterization (Langacker 1999).

The contrast between (51) and (52) also reflects different ways of construing a particular situation.

(52) *John gave the book to Mary.*   (Lee 2001: 2)

(53) *John gave Mary the book.*   (Lee 2001: 2)

The traditional view assumes that these two sentences have the same meaning and the structural difference has no consequence in semantics. The transformational grammar claims that these two sentences are derived from the same underlying structure through formal rules and that the difference between them is a matter of form rather than meaning. However, there is some evidence to indicate that this view is simply not right. One piece of evidence comes from the fact that in some cases only one of the constructions sounds natural. For instance, the sentence *John gave the fence a new coat of paint* is perfectly acceptable but it would be odd to say *John gave a new coat of paint to the fence* (Langacker 1990: 14). These differences indicate that the two sentences in (51) and (52) have to do with different ways of construing the same situation and on some occasions only one mode of construal is appropriate and natural.

3.6 *Perspective*

One factor which is involved in alternative construals has to do with perspective. Langacker (1990) claims that instead of presenting a neutral conception of the situation described, many expressions invoke a conception that embodies a particular viewing arrangement. The effects of such an arrangement imposed on a given situation constitute an inherent aspect of the semantic value of a linguistic expression. The term 'perspective' subsumes several aspects such as 'orientation' and 'vantage point' (or viewpoint). The importance of orientation is quite obvious in the case of *left* and *right* as contrasted in (53) and (54), the use of which is determined by the direction in which the speaker, the listener, or some other viewer faces (cf. Vandeloise 1984; Langacker 1990).

(54) *Turn right at the next corner.*

(55) *John was seated on Mary's left.*

The significance of vantage point (the spot at which the viewer is situated and from which the situation is viewed) is evident from the motion verbs *come* vs. *go*, which indicate motion *to* vs. *away* from the deictic centre usually the speaker or the subject of a sentence. The contrast between the sentences in (56) and (57) has to do with alternative construals as well.

(56) *The path falls steeply into the valley.*   (Lee 2001: 2)

(57) *The path climbs steeply out of the valley.*   (Lee 2001: 2)

Though these two sentences could be employed to depict the same situation, it would be hard for us to say that they express the same meaning. The difference between (56) and (57) involves viewpoint. The viewpoint in (56) is that of someone looking down into the valley while in (57) the viewpoint is that of someone looking up from the valley. For each of the two sentences, a particular viewing position is constructed as part of process of invoking meaning through language. Each sentence has to do with a particular construal of the situation in question and contrasting perspectives contribute to distinct interpretations (Lee 2001).

The relevance of vantage point (or viewpoint) is not restricted to the spatial domain. It can be in a rather more abstract domain, as the two sentences (58) and (59) illustrate.

(58) *John bought the car from Mary.*   (Lee 2001: 3)

(59) *Mary sold the car to John.*   (Lee 2001: 3)

It is obvious that these two sentences describe the same scene, but we would hardly tend to say that they express the same meaning. The contrast between (58) and (59) involves different viewpoints as well. Sentence (58) is an expression of John's viewpoint, but sentence (59) construes the event from the point of view of Mary. Their differences in viewpoints are made more obvious in the contrast of sentences (60) and (61).

(60) *John bought the car from Mary for a good price.* (Lee 2001: 3)

(61) *Mary sold the car to John for a good price.*   (Lee 2001: 3)

It can be inferred that in (60) the price was relatively low; however, sentence (61) indicates that the price was high. This suggests that sentences (58) and (60) are construed for the buy's point of view while sentences (59) and (61) are oriented to that of the seller (Lee 2001).

3.7 Action Chain

Langacker (1990) uses the term *action chain* to refer to "an interaction network which includes a series of energetic interaction thus inducing a reaction whereby it in turn transfers energy to a third, and so on indefinitely" (1990: 215). Typically, the coverage of a clause is limited to certain facets of its interactive network. In a prototypical transitive clause, the profiled process constituting an action chain originates with a canonical agent - volitional energy source and ends with a canonical patient - energy sink (Langacker 1990: 215).

In energetic interactions involving an *instrument* to form an action chain, it is often the case that three participants fall into the scope of predication of a finite clause. The three participants instantiate the canonical agent (ag), instrument (instr) and patient (pat) roles, as Figure 3.3 illustrates.

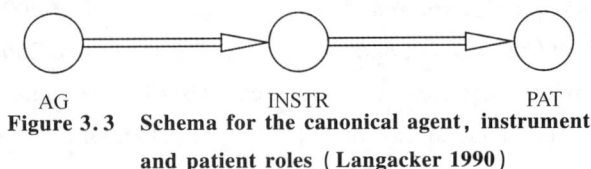

AG   INSTR   PAT

Figure 3.3   Schema for the canonical agent, instrument and patient roles (Langacker 1990)

Prototypically, the agent is chosen to be the subject and the patient is chosen to be the object. The subject is considered to be at the "head" of the profiled portion of the action chain and it lies the farthest "upstream" in the energy flow. On the other hand, the object is at the tail of the profiled portion of the action chain and it occupies the farthest position "downstream" in the flow (Langacker 1990).

3.8 Lexicon and Syntax

It is common practice for linguists to maintain the distinction between syntax and lexicon. Likewise, it is not uncommon for us to come across the recurrent issue of whether a given construction is to be handled in the domain of syntax or in that of the lexicon. The notion of lexicon as an appendix of the grammar or as a list of basic irregularities is not a new one. "The lexical component was dedicated for use as a repository for recalcitrant phenomena that were originally considered syntactic but refused to obey certain preconceived ideas about that syntax should be like" (Langacker 1987: 26). Syntax was deemed to be the domain of generality and regularity containing productive rules to produce fully predictable linguistic expressions. Anything falling short of these standards was relegated to the domain of lexicon which is associated with irregularity, idiosyncrasy, and lists (Langacker 1987). However, this deeply ingrained and widely accepted concept of syntax has very little empirical foundation. There is no a priori reason for us to believe that grammatical constructions can be divided neatly into groups on the basis of generality. There are no factual grounds that the regular aspects of language structure can be separated neatly in any meaningful way from the irregular ones (Langacker 1987).

CG claims that there is no meaningful distinction between grammar and lexicon. Lexicon and syntax form a continuum of symbolic structures. They differ along various parameters, but it is arbitrary to divide them into separate components (Langacker 1987). Langacker (1987) believes that if the lexicon has any content, it refers to fixed expressions, and primarily those that are less than fully compositional. Many expressions that meet these conditions display internal grammatical organization and some of them even display obvious syntactic properties. Thus, CG posits a gradation uniting lexicon, morphology, and syntax. Any strict dichotomy based on novelty, generality and size of expressions is rejected (Langacker 1987). What seems categorical is really a matter of degree.

3.9 *Schematic Representation of a Transitive Event*

Participant sharing is a common phenomenon in multi-verb constructions in Mandarin. To serve as background for schematic representations for shared participant constructions, I would like to pictorially represent an event based on a Langacker-style notation. A canonical transitive event (e. g. ' She ate vegetables. ') which features a relation (⟶) between two event participants ($(P_i)(P_j)$) can be represented as in Figure 3.4:

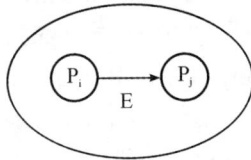

Figure 3.4 A canonical transitive event (Rice 1987a)

A transitive event with an omitted but implied object (e. g. ' She ate. ') can be presented in Figure 3.5. The dashed oval in the figure represents an implied object.

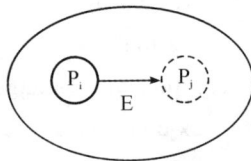

Figure 3.5 A transitive event with an omitted but implied object (Rice 1987a)

Figure 3.4 and Figure 3.5 have featured a shared base with different profiling. In Figure 3.4, both participants are given prominence, but in Figure 3.5, only one participant is profiled.

Chapter Four

The Present Analysis

The present analysis is largely based on iconicity in language. The basic assumption of the iconicity principle in language is that "linguistic forms are frequently the way they are because, like diagrams, they resemble the conceptual structure they are used to convey" (Haiman, 1985: 7). In other words, "grammatical structure is an iconic reflection of conceptual structure" (Newmeyer, 1992: 759). Take iconicity of Complexity as an example. "The idea that linguistic complexity reflects conceptual complexity has long been an important aspect of markedness theory. Marked forms and structures are typically both structurally more complex (or at least longer) and semantically more complex than unmarked ones" (Newmeyer, 1992: 763). Thus, Jakobson (1965: 29-30) observed that "in various Indo-European languages, the positive, comparative, and superlative degrees of adjectives show a gradual increase in the number of phonemes ... There are languages where the plural forms are distinguished from the singular by an additional morpheme, whereas, according to Greengerg, there is no language in which this relation would be reserve".

4.1 *Three Iconically Based Semantic Principles*

In order to capture all the characteristics of true Mandarin Chinese SVCs, a set of operational criteria which go beyond syntax are proposed in this study. The theoretical grounding for classifying Mandarin SVCs is the following three iconically based semantic principles: **temporal** sequence and **scope** as first proposed in Tai (1985), **shared participants**, and **situational dependence**. These three semantic principles all play a role in construing Mandarin multi- verbal expressions.

4.1.1 *Principle of Temporal Sequence and Scope*

The Principle of Temporal Sequence, which is based on iconicity, holds that "the relative word order between two syntactic units is determined by the temporal order of the state which they represent in the conceptual world" (Tai, 1985:50). Chinese is a near isolating language with very few markers of tense and temporal relations. A lot of semantic functions are indicated by word order. Even without overt temporal markers, Chinese sentences can be interpreted appropriately and unambiguously because the default interpretation is based on the iconicity of temporal sequence (Chan, 1997a). Therefore, in Mandarin SVCs, interpretation with regard to temporal sequence between two verbal phrases should be based on the linear order of these phrases.

(62) a. *Ta* **mai** *piao* **jin** **qu.**

　　　3SG **buy** ticket **enter** **go**

　　　'S/he bought a ticket to go in. '

　　b. *Ta* **jin** *qu mai* *piao.*

　　　3SG **enter** **go buy** ticket

　　　'S/he went in to buy a ticket. '

(63) *Women* **jin** *dianyingyuan* **kan** *dianying.*

　　　We **enter** cinema **see** movie

　　　'We went into the cinema to see a film. '

The two VPs in (62) and (63) have a consecutive interpretation based on the iconicity principle of Temporal Sequence. In (62a), the subject first bought the ticket and only then would be allowed to go into the cinema while the alternate order in (62b) yields a different interpretation: the subject first went in and then it was possible for him/her to achieve the aim: buying a ticket. In sentence (63), in order to see a film "we" should first go into the cinema. Therefore, the linearity of the events in these two example sentences is determined by the temporal order of the state in the conceptual world: the first event must precede the second one. Moreover, if these two events are discrete, the first one should be completed before the second one (Chan, 1998).

The Principle of Temporal Scope claims that "if the conceptual state represented by a syntactic unit X falls within the temporal scope of the conceptual state represented by a syntactic unit Y, the word order is YX" (Tai, 1985:60). If two VPs conform to the Principle of Temporal Scope they often suggest a circumstantial, if not purposive interpretation. Consider the following two examples:

(64) *Women*   ***kai***   *hui*   ***taolun***   *ne*   *ige*   *wenti.*

     We   **open**   meeting   **discuss**   that   CL   problem

     'We discussed that problem in the meeting. '

(65) *Ta*   ***shang***   *ke*   ***xuexi***   *yingyu.*

     3SG   **attend**   lesson **learn**   English

     'S/he attended classes to learn English. '

In (64) and (65), the two events are dependent on each other in the sense that the second event is the direct consequence of the first and the second event occurs either simultaneously with the first or it falls within the temporal frame of the first. In sentence (64), the event X *taolun neige wenti* 'discuss that problem' occurs within the temporal scope of the event Y *kai hui* 'hold a meeting' and in sentence (65), the event X *xuexi yingyu* 'learn English' happens within the event Y *shang ke* 'attending lessons'. According to the Principle of Temporal Scope, a syntactic unit with a smaller temporal scope should follow the unit with a larger scope. This principle plays an important role in determining the linearity of verbs in SVCs having a circumstantial (also purposive) interpretation. The word order of the serial verbs in this type of SVC should abide by the principle of temporal scope. It follows that the first event serving as the circumstance has a larger temporal scope than (or at least as large as) the second verb phrase (Chan, 1997).

4.1.2 *Principle of Shared Participants*

The Principle of Shared Participants, grounded on Iconicity of Distance, refers to the phenomenon in which two verbs share at least one participant. The shared participant(s) could be the subject or both the subject and the object in some cases. The omission of the participant(s) between two verb phrases could suggest a closer relationship between them. Iconicity of distance assumes that "the linguistic distance between expressions corresponds to the conceptual distance between them " (Haiman, 1983: 782). As an illustration, lexical causatives (e. g. kill) tend to convey a more direct causation than periphrastic causatives (e. g. cause to die). In the same vein, Mandarin Chinese multi-verbal expressions with or without a subject between two or more verb phrases could suggest different degrees of conceptual distance between them.

(66) *Ta*   *kai*   *luyinji*,   *ta*   *changge.*

3SG   **turn on**   the recorder,   3SG   **sing**

'S/he turned on the recorder and he sang. '

(67) *Ta*   *kai*   *luyinji*   *changge.*

3SG   **turn on**   the recorder   **sing**

'S/he turned on the recorder to sing. '

In (66), the presence of the subject between the two VPs suggests a coordination interpretation rather than a purposive interpretation. It is more likely that there is no situational interdependence between these two events. However, the absence of the subject between the two VPs in (67) suggests less distance between them and a purposive interpretation is preferred in this sentence. Sharing participants is one of the necessary and important characteristics of SVCs in Mandarin Chinese.

4.1.3 *Principle of Situational Dependence*

The Principle of Situational Dependence is defined as an

interdependent relationship between two VPs such as a relationship of means and aims or cause and effect. Because of the interdependence between serial verbs, verbs in such syntactic constructions are strung together in list-like fashion, one after another, but constituent a single grammatical unit. Often the information status of the constituents of the serial construction is reduced, and the separate verbs do not denote individuated events (Frawley, 1992).

(68) *Ta*   *meitian*   **paobu**   **duanlian**   *shenti.*

     3SG   everyday   **run**   **exercise**   body

     'S/he runs to exercise everyday'.

(69) *Ta*   *meitian*   *zaoshang*   **mai** cai   **shang**   *ban.*

     3SG   everyday   morning   **buy** food   **go**   work

     'S/he buys food and goes to work every morning'.

In identifying real SVCs, the principles of Temporal Sequence and Shared Participants are necessary, but not sufficient. In (68), the two VPs-*paobu* 'run' and *duanlian shenti* 'exercise body' bear an interdependent relationship, that is, the purpose of running is for exercising. Sentence (68) complies with the three principles proposed in this study and thus, can be rightfully called an SVC. On the other hand, sentence (69) observes the Principles of Temporal Sequence and Shared Participants in that the two VPs share an argument (the subject) and it is most likely that *mai cai* 'buy food' takes place before *shang ban* 'go to work'. However, there is no situational interdependence between the two VPs, and therefore, it can not be classified as a real SVC.

4.2 *Conceptual Event*

Since my approach proposes that there is a connection between grammatical structure and cognition so that one can link a canonical SVC to a single (or unitary) complex event and that there are degrees of event integration which involves complex events, it would be helpful to define simple and complex events. Events can be simple or complex depending on how many temporal phases they contain and how the speaker conceptualizes the event as a whole. Simple events will be defined as being construed as having a single phase, while complex events will be assumed to be construed as containing more than one phase (c. f. Van Valin & LaPolla 1997; Langacker 2008). Whether simple or complex, all events have a core component—the main activity—which is usually highlighted and salient (Grimshaw 1990). If an event is only composed of a core verbal component and is construed to have one phase, it is deemed a simple event, as in (70):

(70) *Zhe   tiao   du   she   si   le.*

This   CL   poisonous   snake   **die**   PERF

' This poisonous snake died. '

However, in addition to the main element (the activity phase), an event could be construed to have an inception phase and/or termination phase, with the former serving as a preparatory stage and the latter usually signaling a resultative stage of the main activity. Thus, one verb can signal the core phase of an event while another verb can allude to an onset or outcome phase. If more than one phase is involved and expressed in the event, it necessarily becomes a complex event.

An action or an activity can cause a termination, fulfillment, or change of state—that is, a result. An action and its result can form a macro event (Talmy 2000). For example, the death of a poisonous snake could be the result of some action. People could kill a snake by taking some action such as beating or striking it. Speakers can choose sentence forms to reflect the construal of the event as having one or multiple phases that they wish to communicate. The death of the snake could be construed to be a result phase for the action phase of striking, as the example in (71) conveys:

(71) *Ta   da   si   le   yi   tiao   du   she.*

3SG   **strike**   **die**   PERF   one   CL   poisonous   snake.

'S/he stroke a poisonous snake dead.'

The sentence in (71) is an expression of the speaker's construal of the event as having multiple phases. The expression is chosen by the speaker to present the event as having two purposively related phases or stages for the purposes of communication.

In the action of killing a snake, people could take a weapon such as a stick and then use it to strike the snake. Thus, the event of taking a stick can be construed as a preparatory stage (inception phase) for the purpose of striking the snake as in (72):

(72) Ta   **na**   bang   **da**   du   she.

3SG   **take**   stick   **strike**   poisonous   snake.

'S/he took a stick to strike a poisonous snake.'

In addition to the core component, a description of an event could include both an inception phase and a termination phase as (73) illustrates:

(73) Ta   **na**   bang   **da**   si le   du   she.

3SG   **take** stick   **strike** **die** PERF   poisonous   snake.

'S/he took a stick to strike a poisonous snake dead.'

A complex event consisting of more than one phase usually displays, to varying degrees, situational interdependence or semantic relatedness between its component phases. Means and aims or cause and effect are two common types of situational interdependence phenomena conveyed in a complex event. Event integration refers to the intergration of two or more component events into a complex event with two or more corresponding phases (Talmy 2000). Such integration is closely related to situational interdependence. The notion of situational interdependence is scalar and it involves a continuum linking two extremes: one in which the two events are wholly independent as in (74) and the other in which the two events have coalesced into a single event as in (75).

(74) Ta   meitian   **xie**   xin   **hui**   ke.

3SG everyday   write   letter   receive   visitor

'S/he writes letters (and) receives visitors everyday. '

(75) *Ta*   ***sha***   ***si***   *le*   *zhu.*

3SG   perform the action of killing   die   PERF   pig

'S/he killed the pig. '

In fact, some multi-verb sequences express a single event with multiple phases (two sub-events) under an umbrella of one macro event (Talmy 2000), while others express instead two events each being construed to have only one phase. Table 4. 1 illustrates the correspondence between different phases and types of event.

Table 4.1   **Correspondence between different phases and types of events**

Phases	Type of events
core phase	simple event
inception phase + core phase	complex event
core phase + termination phase	complex event
inception phase + core phase + termination phase	complex event
core phase + core phase	2 separate events

However, most multi-verb sequences in Mandarin occupy the conceptual space between complete event autonomy and complete event integration. The two sub-events in many of these multi-verb sequences are integrated semantically in some way to form a complex event and they are causally or consequentially related to various degrees. Like many other linguistic units—all of which are graded phenomena (e. g., Langacker 1987, 1991, 2008), multi-verb sequences display a continuum of event integration/independence. By analyzing such so-called troublesome and ill-understood sequences from the perspective of event integration/independence, all types of multi-verb sequences can be reasonably accounted for.

4.3 Laying Out the Event Conflation Continuum

Loosely, the three principles proposed in this study reflect whether the sequenced VPs in question share a temporal window, event participants, or reflect some other kind of conceptual unity. The first two principles are binary while the third principle is scalar. The notion of situational interdependence involves a continuum linking two extremes: one in which the two verbs (events) are wholly independent as in the case of coordination given in (1) and the other in which the two verbs (events) have coalesced into a single event as in the case of VV compounds given in (5). Figure 4.1 illustrates the continuum of event (in)dependence and the relative locations of the five construction types in (1) - (5) in question on the continuum:

Non SVC   **SVC**

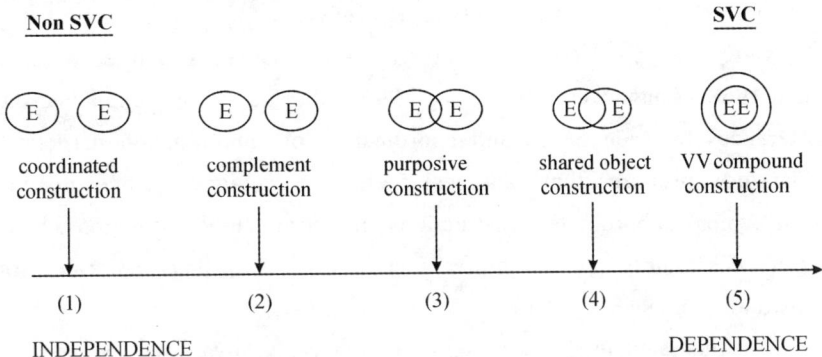

| coordinated construction | complement construction | purposive construction | shared object construction | VV compound construction |

(1)   (2)   (3)   (4)   (5)

INDEPENDENCE   DEPENDENCE

Figure 4.1   Correlation between event dependence and SVC status

In Figure 4.1 the distance or the overlapping between two ovals (circles) in each construction indicates the relative separateness or integration of the two events. Coordinated clause constructions represent the independence of two events while VV compound constructions represent the complete event conflation. The greater overlapping between the two events in shared object constructions than that in purposive complement constructions suggests a tighter relationship.

However, the 5 constructions are a matter of construal. According to communicative needs, speakers can manipulate the kind of interpretation by different means such as the absence or presence of the aspectual particle *le*, the resumptive third person(s) *ta(men)* or certain prosodic elements like stresses or pauses. For example, the absence of the third person singular *ta* from the two VPs as in (66) would change a coordination interpretation to a purposive interpretation as in (67).

4.4 *Event Structure of Coordination, Subordination, and SVCs*

In the literature, there has been much debate over whether SVCs involve coordinate structures or subordinate structures or both; that is, some analyses advocate for the former and others for the latter (e. g. , Li & Thompson 1973; Stewart 2001). However, a few linguists assert that SVCs are not typical coordinate or typical subordinate structures (e. g. , Chao 1968; Langacker 1991; Song 1992) , but no one has explained the differences between SVCs and coordination or subordination in detail. This study proposes that canonical SVCs have unique features distinct from typical subordinate constructions or coordinate constructions. The differences mainly lie in their respective event profiling—an aspect of construal (Langacker 1991).

As illustrated in the next series of diagrams, ovals will be used to represent individual events and line thickness to represent degree of profiling or cognitive salience. In typical coordinate constructions, as in (76) neither individual clausal profile overrides the other at the higher level of organization. The two clauses in this sentence are co-equal and they do not stand in a main/subordinate clause relationship. Thus, each clause has the main clause status.

(76) *Ta*   *meitian*   ***duanlian***   *shenti*   ***xuexi***   *hanyu.*

     3SG   everyday   exercise   body   study   Chinese

' S/he exercises his/her body (and) studies Chinese everyday. '

In a typical case of coordination, each conjunct is separate and equally profiled, as indicated by the bold line in Figure 4. 2. Therefore, typical coordinate constructions have two processual profiles (Langacker 1991). The two clauses in such constructions are independent and there is no situational inter-dependence between them. Very often, there is no temporal sequential relation between them either.

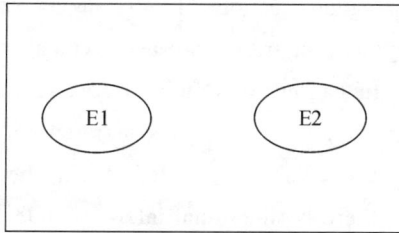

Figure 4. 2   Event structure of coordination

By contrast, in a typical subordinate construction, there is usually only one main clause, as illustrated by the bold oval in Figure 4. 3, in addition to a subordinate clause, as illustrated by the dotted oval. A main clause is the profile determinant and lends its profile to the composite structure of a multi-clausal expression (Langacker 1991: 436). A subordinate clause is defined as one " whose profile is overridden by that of a main clause" (Langacker 1991:436) at the composite structure, represented in Figure 4. 3 by the bigger oval which subsumes both E1 and E2.

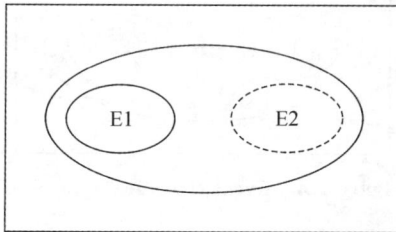

Figure 4. 3   Event structure of subordination

In a typical complement or subordinate clause construction, the main clause and the subordinate clause combine directly. The main clause determines the profile of the overall structure as in (77). The sentence designates the process of confessing, not of doing something wrong.

(77) *Ta* *chengren* *zuo* *cuo* *le*.

3SG confess do wrong PERF

'He confessed that he had done something wrong.'

Finally, what is called a canonical SVC has its own characterization, distinct from the typical coordination and typical subordination cases (Langacker 1991). In canonical Mandarin SVCs, two or more content verbs (or phrases) of equal status are incorporated within a single clause. In Figure 4.4, both events are profiled as in the typical coordinate structure. However, there is situational inter-dependence between the two events, indicated by a bold line which connects them. As in the SVC *qu chi fan* 'go eat a meal', the two verbs represent successive temporal but interdependent phases. These two purposively related phases are construed to be one overall event represented by the bigger bold oval which subsumes both E1 and E2. Thus, typical SVCs profile a single process comprising two or more separately coded phases. These phases join to form a composite verb (or verb phrase) which acts as the profile determinant for a clause (Langacker 1991).

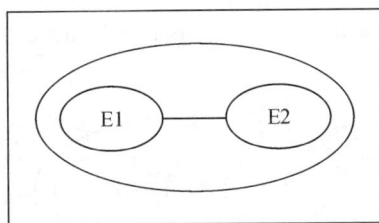

Figure 4.4   Event structure of an SVC

Cognitive Grammar provides us useful mechanisms for describing differences between event structures such as coordination, subordination, and serialization. It enables us to discern the similarities and differences among them. In the examples just cited, each of these three general categories of constructions involves two events (or sub-events). The two events (or sub-events) are both profiled in coordinate constructions and in SVCs, since both (sub)-events are raised to a distinctive level of prominence in these two constructions. However, as shown in Figure 4.2 and Figure 4.4, the two events in typical coordinate constructions are independent and there is no necessary semantic relation between them, while the two events in SVCs are semantically inter-dependent and are construed as two phases under the single umbrella of a macro event. A macro event is a kind of complex event since it consists of at least two phases. In subordinate constructions, as indicated in Figure 4.3, only one event denoted by the main event is profiled and the other event denoted by the subordinate clause is not profiled. This asymmetrical schema usually serves as a representation of complementation or modification relations.

4.5 *Morphosyntactic and Prosodic Tests of Event Conflation*

When two verbs represent semantically independent events, they could be coded overtly in separate clauses in Mandarin or they are generally interpretable as being coordinated even if the two VPs are construed as a sequenced string without any syntactic marker, such as *he* 'and'.

(78) a. *Zhangsan **da**-le   lanqiu,   Lisi **kan**-le   dianying.*

　　　Zhangsan **play**-ASP   basketball, Lisa **see**-ASP   film

　　　'Zhangsan played basketball and Lisi saw a film. '

　　*b. *Zhangsan **da**-le   lanqiu   he Lisi **kan**-le   dianying.*

　　　Zhangsan **play**-ASP   basketball and Lisa **see**-ASP film

The two events in (78a) are wholly independent though they might be coincidental; accordingly, the two verb phrases have different subjects and are coded in separate clauses. The coordinate relation between the two clauses can be inferred from the context. However, in (78b) the addition of the conjunction *he* 'and' leads to a redundancy and the resulting sentence is ungrammatical. This suggests that the omission of the conjunction '*he*' is obligatory when the two events in the two conjuncts (clauses) with different subjects are wholly unrelated. One point about the use of the connector *he* 'and' in Mandarin Chinese should be mentioned. English speakers tend to use the connector 'and' more frequently than Chinese speakers do. Furthermore, it is not uncommon for English speakers to use this connector to coordinate two sentences while Chinese speakers rarely use *he* to connect two clauses. The main function of the connector *he* in Mandarin is to coordinate two phrases or two words rather than two clauses. It does, however, connect two independent clauses which share a subject. In such cases, the iconicity of Distance Principle is clearly at work. If two VPs have the same subject as in (79a) it is possible to omit the second subject and to construe the two VPs in one clause as a case of coordination connected by *he* as in (79b). The conflation of two clauses into one sentence by omitting the identical subject in the second VP signals a tighter connection between the two conjuncts. Furthermore, if the connector *he* is omitted as in (79c) a much tighter connection could be suggested in suitable contexts and, as a result, an SVC interpretation is possible.

(79) a. *Zhangsan **da**-le   lanqiu,   Zhangsan **kan**-le   dianying.*

        Zhangsan **play**-ASP basketball, Zhangsan **see**-ASP film

        'Zhangsan played basketball, Zhangsan saw a film. '

   b. *Zhangsan **da**-le   lanqiu   he   **kan**-le   dianying.*

        Zhangsan **play**-ASP basketball and **see**-ASP film

        'Zhangsan played basketball and saw a film. '

   c. *Zhangsan **da**   lanqiu   **kan**   dianying.*

        Zhangsan **play**   basketball **see**   film

'Zhangsan played basketball (so that) he could see a film. '

When two verbs share a subject, the presence or absence of the conjunction 'he' could affect the possible interpretation of the sentence in certain contexts. In (79b) the presence of 'he' indicates that the two verbs are independent and can only be interpreted as a case of coordination not as an SVC. However, the absence of the conjunction 'he' between the two verbs as in (79c) could lead to an SVC construal in suitable contexts. In (79c), if Zhangsan's playing basketball is for the purpose of getting a ticket to see a film, the sentence could be interpreted as an SVC because then these two VPs are somewhat dependent. On the other hand, if Zhangsan's playing basketball has nothing to do with his getting a ticket to see a film, the construction is likely to be interpreted as coordination. In that case, (79b) is preferred to (79c). Even if in a neutral context, when there is no pause between the two VPs in (79c) it is more likely for Mandarin speakers to interpret this sentence as a purposive construction.

If this is the case, then how could two sequenced VPs be classified as a SVC in Mandarin? If two sequenced VPs bear any kind of interrelationship, they are eligible for interpretation as a SVC and can manifest the attendant morphosyntax or prosody of SVCs. In short, the two sequenced VPs either do or do not pass the following tests:

(a) the *le* test (this perfective particle affixes to all main verbs or verb complexes to signal completion of (wholistic) event; verbs in an SVC share a single *le* particle while in non-SVCs each verb could be marked by *le*) ;

(b) the multiple temporal adverb test (SVCs tend to allow a single temporal adverb specification, while non-SVCs can allow several) ;

(c) the *ta* test (a resumptive 3SG subject *ta*, can surface between coordinated VPs which share a subject, but not between the verbs of an SVC) ;

(d) the stress placement test (generally, each verb in coordinated VPs receives main stress while in an SVC only the head verb does);

(e) the reversibility test (two VPs in non-SVCs could be reversible without affecting the meaning of the sentence while reversal of two VPs in SVCs results in either unacceptable sentences or completely changing the meaning of the expression);

(f) the *ba* test (in Mandarin, an object can be preposed to the pre-verbal position triggered by the object marker ba. In coordination, each VP can allow *ba* to prepose its object while a typical SVC can only allow one *ba* to prepose the object in the main verb);

(g) the pause test (a pause is possible or even necessary in two VPs in non-SVCs).

Table 4. 2 Some syntactic and prosodic diagnostics

for determining event (in)dependence

THE SEVEN TESTS	SVC	non-SVC
I. *le* test	one	multiple
II. temporal adverb test	one	multiple
III. *ta* test	prohibited	possible
IV. stress test	one	multiple
V. reversibility test	prohibited or change in meaning	possible
VI. *ba* test	one	multiple
VII. pause test	prohibited	possible or necessary

The seven tests are grounded on the three principles proposed in this study and on the overall assumption that the two VPs in an SVC signal one main conceptual event. The *le* test and the stress test are mainly grounded on the Principle of Situational Dependence, which suggests that more often than not the main verb attracts stress and the perfective particle *le* suffixes to the main verb or verb complexes. The temporal adverb test, the *ba* test, and the pause test as well are both motivated by the Principle of Situational Dependence and the overall assumption of a SVC being one conceptual unit. In SVCs, "the time of the events in sequence is frequently reduced, with time attributed only to the entire construction: that is, to the event that has full information status" (Frawley, 1992: 143). The *ta* test is based on the Principle of Shared Participants, which implies that sharing an argument is one of the necessary and essential properties of SVCs. The reversibility test is motivated by the Principle of Temporal Sequence, which indicates that the order of VPs in SVCs should reflect the temporal order of the events in the conceptual world. Basically, these seven tests are suggested to diagnose whether two sequenced VPs demonstrate the properties of one unified conceptual event or two discrete conceptual events. Consequently, if these tests indicate that a given construction is more like one unified conceptual event, it can qualify as an SVC, otherwise it is better to be analyzed as a non-SVC. In the next chapter, I will discuss sentence types like those first exemplified in (1) - (5) and show how they meet or fail to meet the seven aforementioned tests.

Chapter Five

The Five Constructions
and the Seven Tests

5.1 *Coordinate Constructions*

5.1.1 *Schematic Representation*

The event independence of coordinate constructions can be represented schematically. The schematic representation of coordination can be illustrated in the following figure:

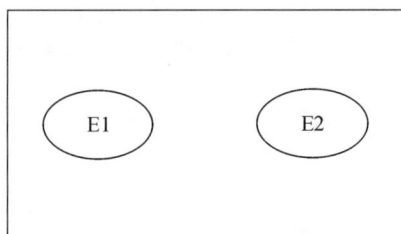

Figure 5.1   The conceptual independence of adjacent events

Figure 5.1 illustrates independence between two events as denoted by two unconjoined but adjacent VPs. In such cases, they are construed as instances of coordination and reflect two separated conceptual events. Coordinated structures display the limiting case of complete event autonomy on one end of the continuum of event independence, as illustrated in Figure 4.1.

5.1.2 *Application of Tests*

The sentence in (80) has a coordination interpretation and could be considered as a prototypical non-SVC.

(80) *Ta   meitian* **duanlain** *shengti* **xuexi**   *yingyu*
     S/he   everyday **exercise** body   **study**   English
     ' S/he does exercises and studies English everyday. '

In (80) the two VPs are neither temporally nor existentially bounded and there is no interdependence between them. In this example, both the subject and the coordination marker *he* are omitted. The omission of *he* may cause ambiguity in its interpretation. However, the semantic properties of the two VPs can disambiguate how it is interpreted. Normally, we cannot discern any kind of interdependence between *duanlain shengti* ' exercise body ' and *xuexi yingyu* ' study English ' in this sentence and its interpretation should be one of mere coordination. Two VPs in a coordinated relationship are categorically not SVCs. As a result, they do not pass any of the morphosyntactic and prosodic tests for SVCs proposed in this study. The critical forms are given in bold in the examples below.

(81) (a) *LE* **TEST**—2 possible

   Ta   jintian   duanlain-le   shengti   xuexi-le   yingyu
   S/he   today   exercise-**ASP** body   study-**ASP** English

(b) **ADVERB TEST**—2 possible

   *Ta   **meitian**   duanlain   **meitian**   xuexi   yingyu*
   S/he **everyday** exercise   **everyday** study   English

(c) *TA* **INSERTION**—possible

   Ta   meitian   duanlain shengti **ta**   *meitian   xuexi yingyu.*
   S/he everyday exercise body   s/**he** everyday study English

(d) **STRESS TEST**—multiple possible

   Ta   meitian   'duanlain   shengti   'xuexi   yingyu
   S/he everyday **exercise** body   **study** English

(e) **REVERSIBILITY TEST**—reversible without changing
essential meaning

*Ta   meitian   **xuexi** yingyu **duanlain** shengti.*
S/he everyday **study** English **exercise** body

(f) *BA* **TEST**—2 possible

*Ta   jintian **ba** shengti duanlain le **ba** yingyu xue   le*
S/he today **ba** body   exercise ASP **ba** English study ASP

(g) **PAUSE TEST**—pause possible

Ta   meitian   duanlain shengti, (...) xuexi yingyu.
S/he everyday exercise body   study English

5.1.3 *Discussion*

The application of the seven tests indicates that coordinate
constructions fail to pass any of the tests for SVCs. They allow two
temporal adverbials and two *le* attachments. Two stresses and two *ba*
particles are possible in such constructions. *Ta* insertions, reversibility
and pauses are all permitted in coordinated constructions. These properties
demonstrate that the events in coordinated clause constructions are
separate and independent.

One point I want to emphasize is the reversibility of non SVCs versus
SVCs. An SVC differs from a coordinated verbal expression in that the
latter can be reversible without affecting the propositional value of the
sentence while the reversal of SVCs will result in either an ungrammatical
sentence or in a completely different interpretation. Consider the
coordinated constructions in (82) and compare them to the SVCs in
(83):

(82) *a. Women   meitian   **xie   xin   hui   ke.***
       We   everyday **write letter receive visitor**
       ' We write letters and receive visitors everyday. '

       b. *Women   meitian   **hui   ke   xie   xin.***
       We   everyday **receive visitor write letter**

'We write letters and receive visitors everyday. '

(83) a. *Women* **cheng** *feiji* **qu** *Beijing.*

We   **take**   plane   **go**   Beijing

'We take a plane to go to Beijing. '

b. *Women* **qu** *Beijing* **cheng** *feiji.*

We   **go**   Beijing   **take**   plane

'We go to Beijing to take a plane. '

The two verbal phrases in (82a) *xiexin huike* 'write letters and receive visitors' can be reversed as *huike xiexin* 'receive visitors and write letters', as in (82b), without affecting the main propositional content of the sentence. However, the two orders in (83) obviously suggest different interpretations entirely (Chao, 1968: 326). In (83a), the purpose of taking a plane is go to Beijing while in (83b), the purpose of going to Beijing is take a plane there.

5.2 *Complement Constructions*

5.2.1 *Schematic Representation*

As stated previously, the string $[NP_1\ V\ (NP_2)\ V\ ...]$ is at least 5-way ambiguous. What then, is the possible relationship in terms of co-reference between NP_1 and NP_2. There are two possibilities between them as the indices indicate: $[NP_i\ V\ (NP_i)\ V]$ or $[NP_i\ V\ (NP_j)\ V]$. Consequently, the kind of clausal complement following V_1 is variable. It could be an overt clause if a subject occurs between two VPs; otherwise, it could be an embedded clause. On the other hand, which items can take clausal complements are largely determined by their semantic properties. The candidate verbs for V_1 in such cases are lexically limited and they are mainly of two kinds: (1) VERBS OF COMMUNICATION such as *shuo* 'say', *baogao* 'report', *chengren* 'admit', *gongren* 'confess' *fouren* 'deny' and (2) VERBS OF COGNITION such as *zhidao* 'know', *juede* ' feel ' , *gandao* ' think ' , *renshidao* ' realize ' . In contrast, the candidate verbs for V$_2$ are relatively open. Virtually any kind of verb or event can be the complement of communication or cognition.

In the case of complement clauses following cognitive and communicative verbs, when the two NPs are not identical it is impossible for the two VPs to share a participant. The resulting sentences will be matrix sentences containing overt complement clauses and they should definitely be ruled out from true SVC status as the following two examples illustrate:

(84) *Ta shuo ni zuo cuo le.*
   S/he say you do wrong ASP
   ' S/he said that you had done something wrong. '

(85) *Ta juede ni zuo cuo le.*
   3SG feel you do wrong ASP
   ' S/he felt that you had done something wrong. '

However, when two NPs in preverbal positions are identical for clausal complement constructions like (3) containing cognitive or communicative verbs, NP$_2$ can be construed overtly or covertly. If it is construed overtly, it violates the Principle of Shared Participates as in (86) and (87) because the two VPs in these sentences do not share any participant.

(86) *Ta shuo ta zuo cuo le.*
   3SG say 3SG do wrong ASP
   ' S/he said that s/he had done something wrong. '

(87) *Ta juede ta zuo cuo le.*
   3SG feel 3SG do wrong ASP
   ' S/he felt that s/he had done something wrong. '

If the two NPs are identical it is possible to omit the second NP and the resulting sentences will then conform to the Principle of Shared Participants as (88), (89) and (90) illustrate:

(88) *Ta chengren zuo cuo le.*

3SG   **confess**   **do**   wrong   ASP

' S/he confessed that s/he had done something wrong. '

(89) *Ta*   ***shuo***   ***zuo***   *cuo*   *le.*

3SG   **say**   **do**   wrong   ASP

' S/he said that s/he had done something wrong. '

(90) *Ta*   ***juede***   ***zuo***   *cuo*   *le.*

3SG   **feel**   **do**   wrong   ASP

' S/he felt that s/he had done something wrong. '

In (88) - (90), the two VPs share a participant and the second VP serves as the complement of the first verb, which abides by the Principle of Shared Participants. Then can these sentences be considered as SVCs? The answer is still negative. One of the reasons why these sentences do not qualify as true SVCs is that they violate the Principle of Temporal Sequence.

Thus, the schematic representation of complement constructions containing communicative or cognitive matrix verbs can be illustrated in Figure 5.2:

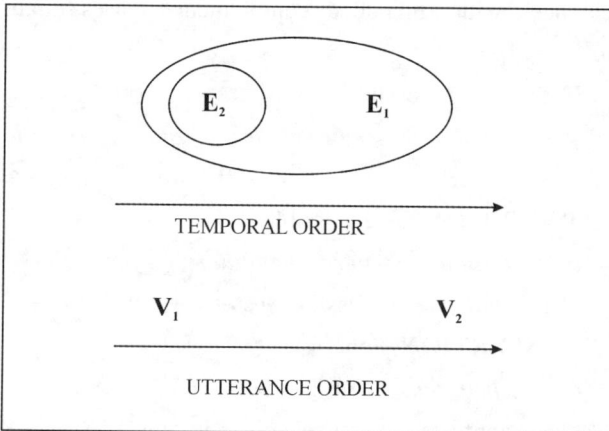

Figure 5.2   Illustration of relative independence of clausal complements

Figure 5.2 shows that EVENT$_2$ denoted by VP$_2$ happened before

EVENT$_1$ denoted by VP$_1$ but syntactically it is coded after EVENT$_1$ as the direction of the arrow indicates. In Figure 5. 2, the circle around EVENT$_2$ indicates the relative independence of this clausal complement, which itself can be considered as a separate event. As (88), (89) and (90) illustrate, EVENT$_2$ happened before EVENT$_1$ and thus EVENT$_2$ is relatively independent from EVENT$_1$ in the sense that EVENT$_2$ had already taken place whether somebody said it, felt it, denied it or the like. Therefore, they do not comply with the Principle of Situational Dependence, and thus, they do not constitute a single unifying event as true SVCs do. Furthermore, these sentences violate the Principle of Temporal Sequence because the relative word order between the two events does not reflect the temporal order of the state in the conceptual world, that is, EVENT$_2$ in these examples happened before EVENT$_1$ but it is coded syntactically after EVENT$_1$.

5.2.2 Application of Tests

Next I would like to apply morphosyntactic and prosodic tests to see whether sentences with embedded complement clauses qualify as true SVCs or not.

(91) (a) *LE TEST*—2 possible

Ta	shuole/ ? chengren	*le*	zuo	cuo	*le.*
S/he	say **ASP**/confess	**ASP**	do	wrong	**ASP**

(b) **ADVERB TEST**—2 possible

Ta	*jintian*	chengren	*zuotian*	zuo	cuo	le.
S/he	**today**	confess	**yesterday**	do	wrong	ASP

(c) *TA INSERTION*—possible

Ta	chengren	*ta*	zuo	cuo	le.
S/he	confess	**s/he**	do	wrong	ASP

(d) **STRESS TEST**—multiple possible

Ta	*'chengren*	(*ta*)	*'zuo*	cuo	le.
S/he	**confess**	(s/he)	**do**	wrong	ASP

(e) **BA** TEST—possible in the complement clause

Ta	chengren	**ba**	na	tiao	gou	da	le
S/he	confess	**OBJ**	that CL		dog	beat	ASP

The following examples demonstrate the application of the reversibility test and the pause test to structures containing clausal complements:

(92) a. *T a* **chengren** (*ta*) **zuo** *cuo* *le*.   (**unpreposed**)

   S/he **confess** (s/he) **do** wrong ASP

b. (*Ta*) **zuo** *cuo* *le*, *ta* **chengren** (**preposed**)

   (S/he) **do** wrong ASP, s/he **confess**

(93) a. *Wo* **juede** *yinggai* *mingtian* **qu** *Beijing*.   (**unpreposed**)

   I **think** should tomorrow **go** Beijing

b. *Yinggai* *mingtian* **qu** *Beijing*, *wo* **juede**.   (**preposed**)

   should tomorrow **go** Beijing, I **think**

In this type of subordination the entire clausal complement (VP_2) can be preposed and the resulting structure is still grammatical. Thus, the focus can be put on the clausal complement. The possibility of preposing the clausal complement shows that the event denoted by the clausal complement can be interpreted as a discrete event.

As for the pause test, when the inter-verbal NP is omitted, it seems not quite acceptable for the pause to occur between two VPs as in (94a); however, when the inter-verbal NP is restored it is quite acceptable to have a pause occurring between the two VPs.

(94) ? a. *Ta* **chengren**, (...) **zuo** *cuo* *le*.

   S/he **confess**, **do** wrong ASP

b. *Ta* **chengren**, (...) *ta* **zuo** *cuo* *le*.

   S/he **confess**, s/he **do** wrong ASP

This shows that constructions like embedded clausal complements cannot completely pass all the tests for non-SVCs proposed in this study though they can pass most of the tests. They are different from coordination cases, however, which are completely independent. There is some relationship between the matrix verb and the subordinate verb in a clausal complement. However, the binding force between the two sequenced VPs — where one serves as the complement to the other — is weak and certainly not as strong as in true SVCs to integrate the two VPs into a single unified conceptual event or a macro event with two parts or phases. Therefore, two VPs manifesting subordination like clausal complements are not really conceptually fused in the way that true SVCs are.

5.2.3 Discussion

The above tests show that in two sequenced VPs with clausal complements, each verb can be marked by *le* and each allows its own temporal adverb specification. Furthermore, the resumptive subject pronoun *ta* can be restored between the two VPs and each verb (or VP) can receive main stress if both events need emphasizing for discourse purposes. The *ba* test is not very relevant for the diagnosis here because there is no NP following V_1 to serve as its object. As a result, there is only one NP to be fronted to the preverbal position in the *ba* construction, which is the object in the embedded clause. However, the possibility of fronting the object in $EVENT_2$ to the preverbal position indicates that $EVENT_2$ (the clausal complement) manifests the characteristics as a separate event.

5.3 *Purposive Constructions*

5.3.1 *Purposive Complements or Separate Clauses*

If two verbs bear a semantic relationship of dependence such as cause and effect or means and aims, they are eligible for being construed as an SVC. However, there are alternative constructions and alternative ways of construing the entire event complex in these cases. Consider the sentences in (95) and (96):

(95) a. *Zhangsan* **mai** *piao* **kan** *dianying.*

Zhangsan **buy** ticket **see** film

'Zhangsan bought a ticket to see a film. '

b. * *Zhangsan* *mai piao* **ta** *kan dianying.*

Zhangsan buy ticket **he** see film

(96) *Zhangsan* *mai* *piao* **yihou** (*ta*) *kan-le* *dianying.*

Zhangsan buy ticket **afterward** (he) see-ASP film

'After Zhangsan bought a ticket he saw a film. '

In (95a) the speaker puts emphasis on the dependent relationship between the two verbs: the purpose of buying a ticket is expressively to see a film. The two verbs are construed as a sequenced string involving the same principal participant without any overt syntactic marker between them. Therefore, they qualify as forming an SVC. When two VPs bear a purposive relationship, the restoration of the resumptive pronoun between them results in an ungrammatical sentence. In (95b), the purpose of buying a ticket is for seeing a film. The connection between the two events is tight and they are causally linked, which makes *ta* ' s/he ' insertion unacceptable. In fact, the insertion of *ta* ' s/he ' in (95b) violates the iconicity Principle of Distance, because such an insertion suggests more distance between the two VPs and a purposive interpretation will no longer hold between them.

On the other hand, in (96) the speaker puts emphasis on the time sequence holding between the two events rather than the causal relationship between them: one event happens after the other and a temporal conjunction is called for. The presence of the overt syntactic marker *yihou* ' after ' disqualifies this structure from being interpreted as an SVC. If two verbs or clauses are highly dependent or they jointly express a single conceptual unit or temporal event, they are likely to be incorporated into one clause as in the case of verb-verb compounds, which will be analyzed in detail in a separate section.

5.3.2 The Three Principles Reflected in Purposive SVCs

When two sequenced VPs bear a purposive relationship, their interpretation should conform to the Principle of Temporal Sequence. Chinese is different from most Indo-European languages in that Chinese has almost no inflections and very few markers for tense or other temporal relations. Accordingly, sentence interpretations are largely based on word order.

The following examples illustrate a purposive interpretation for a construction type (3) multiverbal structure:

(97) *Ta*　　**kai**　　*luyinji*　　**tiaowu**.

　　3SGM　**turn on**　the recorder　**dance**

　　'He turned on the recorder to dance.'

(98) *Ta*　　**mai**　*piao*　**kan**　*dianying*.

　　3SGM　**buy**　ticket　**see**　film

　　'S/he bought a ticket to see a film.'

These sentences have a purposive interpretation whereby the first event is performed in order to achieve the execution of the second. For an SVC to invite a purposive interpretation, it is important that the purpose (i. e. something to be done or carried out) be realizable in the very near future within a certain time frame (Chan, 1998). Usually the first event is conducted before the second and, accordingly, $EVENT_1$ is linearly ordered before $EVENT_2$. In (97) and (98), the first event precedes the second and the performance of the first event is critical to enable the execution of the second.

Being iconic with temporal sequence does not entail that the construction should be considered as an SVC. Interdependence of the two events is also a key factor in distinguishing an SVC from a non-SVC. In the words of Newmeyer, "The more conceptual control a main verb exerts on a complement verb, the more likely the latter is to be incorporated with the former and the less likely a complementizer [or a conceptualizer] is to occur in the embedded clause" (Newmeyer, 1992: 762). In (97), *kai luyinji* 'turn on the recorder' and *tiaowu* 'dance' are largely interdependent; the first event is performed for the purpose of carrying out the second event. The absence or omission of an overt conceptualizer between the two verbs emphasizes their dependence and relatedness. Consequently, the conjunction *he* 'and' is not allowed in such purposive interpretations; otherwise, it would signal no relation between the two events.

On the other hand, if two actions bear no interdependent relationship, for example, his turning on the radio has nothing to do with his dancing, the subject of the second VP in this case cannot be omitted as in (99) even though it is identical to the subject of the first VP.

(99) *Ta*   **kai**   *luyinji*,   *ta*   **tiaowu.**

　　　He   **turn on**   the recorder,   3SGM   **dance**

　　　'He turned on the recorder and he danced. '

Therefore (99) allows a coordination interpretation rather than a purposive interpretation. The two events denoted by their respective clauses at most have a consecutive relationship in that the first event occurs before the second. However, there is no situational interdependence between them such as being causally linked. On the other hand, in order for (99) to allow a purposive interpretation, a purposive connector like *yibian* 'in order that' is usually needed between the two VPs:

(100) *Ta*   *kai*   *luyinji*   **yibian**   *ta*   *neng*   *tiaowu.*

　　　He   turn on   the recorder   **in order that** 3SGM   can   dance

　　　'He turned on the recorder in order that he could dance. '

In order to indicate the purpose of the first action in (100), a connector *yibian* '*in order that*' is called for between the two events. Its presence will result in a finite subordinate clause interpretation. Accordingly, this construction cannot be classified as an SVC.

When two VPs have a purposive interpretation, it is possible for these two verb phrases to share a participant. In distinguishing SVCs from non-SVCs, the Principles of Shared Participants and Temporal Sequence are necessary, but not sufficient. When two verbs which denote two discrete events are independent, a subject is likely to occur between them to allow a coordinated interpretation as in sentence (99). Even if the two verbs share a subject in a coordinated structure, they do not necessarily qualify as an SVC because they may bear no dependent relationship and, accordingly, a coordinate marker can be put between the two verbs. Consider (101):

(101) *Zhangsan   meitian   **kan**   shu   (**he**)   du   bao.*
　　　Zhangsan   everyday **read** book   (**and**) **read**   newspaper
　　　'Zhangsan reads books and newspapers every day.'

In sentence (101), the coordinate conjunction *he* 'and' occurs between the two verbs to indicate the independence of the two actions even though these two VPs share a subject. Based on the meanings of the two VPs in (101), we cannot discern any dependence between them. However, when two verbs bear some kind of relationship of dependence, a subject between them is likely to be omitted if the subject is coreferential or otherwise recoverable from the context. Furthermore, a coordinate conjunction cannot be inserted between them. Otherwise it would result in an ungrammatical sentence or change the meaning of the sentence.

(102) a. **Ta   **mai**   piao   **he**   **jin**   qu*.
　　　　 3SGF **buy**   ticket **and enter go**
　　　　 'She bought a ticket and went in.'

　　　 b. *Ta   mai   piao   **jin**   qu*.
　　　　 3SGF **buy**   ticket   **enter**   **go**
　　　　 'She bought a ticket to go in.'

　　In a word, structures are themselves meaningful. Two verbs with a shared subject denoting two discrete events as in (102a) linked with the coordinate conjunction *he* 'and' suggest a coordination interpretation in that their relationship is independent. On the other hand, the absence of the coordinate marker *he* 'and' as in (102b) makes it possible for them to have a purposive interpretation.

5.3.3 *Schematic Representation*

The schematic representation of SVCs with purposive interpretation can be illustrated in the following figure:

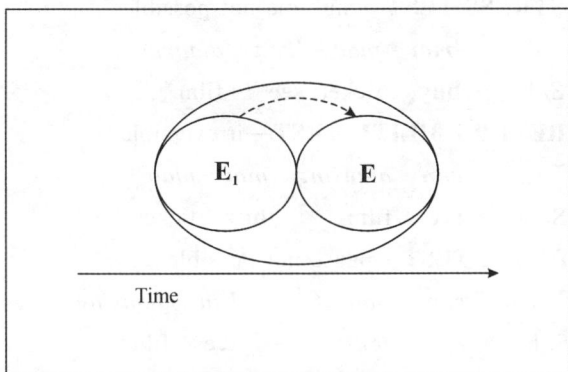

Figure 5.3   Two events causally linked to form a single macro event

Figure 5.3 illustrates a purposive construction. The dotted line between EVENT₁ and EVENT₂ indicates that the two events are causally linked. The big oval encompassing the two small circles suggests that EVENT₁ and EVENT₂ conceptually comprise one unified event. In other words, two micro events with a purposive interpretation can be considered as two different stages of a larger macro event.

5.3.4 *Application of the Tests*

The application of morphosyntactic and prosodic tests proposed in this study shows that sentences with a purposive complement like (3) repeated in (97) can generally pass the SVC tests.

(103) (a) *LE* **TEST**—2 not possible

* Ta	mai	piao	*le*	kan	dianying	*le*.
S/he	*buy*	*ticket*	**ASP**	see	film	**ASP**

(b) **ADVERB TEST**—2 possible, but change the focus

? *Ta*   ***jintian*** *mai* *piao* ***mingtain*** *kan* *dianying.*

S/he   **today** buy ticket **tomorrow** see   film

(c) ***TA* INSERTION**—not possible

Ta   *mai* *piao* *ta*   *kan*   *dianying.*

S/he   buy ticket s/**he** see   film

(d) **STRESS TEST**—multiple not possible

Ta   *'mai* *piao* *'kan* *dianying.*

S/he   **buy**   ticket **see**   film

(e) **REVERSIBILITY TEST**—irreversible

Ta   *kan* *dianying* *mai* *piao.*

S/he   **see** film   **buy** ticket

(f) **PAUSE TEST**—pause not possible

Ta   *mai* *piao*, (⋯) *kan*   *dianying.*

S/he   buy ticket,   see   film

(g) ***BA* TEST**—1 possible

Ta   *mai* *piao* *ba*   *dianying* *kan-le.*

S/he   buy ticket **OBJ** film   see-ASP

(h) ***BA* TEST**—2 not quite possible

? *Ta* *ba*   *piao* *mai-le* *ba*   *dianying* *kan-le.*

S/he   OBJ ticket buy-ASP **OBJ** film   see-ASP

Example (103) with a purposive complement basically allows one *le* attached to the entire event complex and receives only one main stress on the head verb. The two VPs in (103) are causally linked to form a macro event, which makes it impossible to have a pause between them. The restoration of *ta* between the two VPs will either result in an ungrammatical sentence or it will change the meaning of the sentence in a way that a purposive relationship will no longer exist. In that case, it is most likely that the tickets are not for seeing the film but for something else.

If each VP in this structure allows one temporal adverb specification, the focus will be changed from a purposive interpretation to a temporal interpretation. The resulting sentence will be best analyzed as an instance of clause coordination rather than as an SVC. Interestingly, a sentence with a purposive interpretation can either allow one *ba* construction as in (103g) or two as in (103h). However, the meanings of these two sentences could be different. In the sentence with one *ba* construction, the purpose of buying a ticket is unambiguously for seeing a film and such a sentence can be best analyzed as a true SVC. On the other hand, in the sentence with two *ba* constructions the ticket is most likely not for seeing a film and as a result, the two events are not causally connected and such a sentence should be best analyzed as coordinated clauses. On the whole, a structure with a purposive interpretation in which two VPs share a principal participant as their subject manifests the basic properties of one conceptually unified event and they should be classified as a true SVC.

5.3.5 Discussion

SVCs with purposive interpretations differ from constructions with embedded clausal complements in that the former display a contextual entailment while the latter do not. The entailment is grounded on conventional expectations. In our mental schemata (McCabe, 1998), the purpose of buying a ticket is to see a film if these two events are strung together without any syntactic marker. In the same vein, the default (or normal) expectation tells us that the purpose of going into a restaurant is to have dinner there; otherwise, the purpose should be specified. In SVCs with purposive interpretations two events are sheltered under one conceptual umbrella and comprise one macro event. On the other hand, in a construction with a clausal complement like (2) repeated here as (104), the two events are not causally linked and bear no situational dependence.

(104) *Ta* **chengren** (*ta*) ***zuo*** *cuo* *le.*
      3SG **confess** (3SG) **do** wrong ASP

'S/he confessed that s/he had done something wrong. '

In (104) whether the subject did something wrong or not absolutely does not depend on whether s/he denies or confesses it. The concept of his/her doing something wrong is a separate event and V₁ such as *shuo* 'say', *chengren* 'admit, confess', *jianchi* 'insist', *gongren* 'confess' or *fouren* 'deny' bears no interdependent relationship with VP₂ (EVENT₂). Thus, EVENT₂ in a clausal complement construction is defeasible. Therefore, based on the semantic principle of situational interdependence proposed in this study, two VPs sharing a subject with a purposive interpretation qualify as a true SVC while a construction with a clausal complement does not.

5.4 *Double-headed or Shared Object Constructions*

SVCs with shared objects (actually with shared subjects as well) are what Baker (1989) defines as double-headed constructions. In this kind of construction (which I do consider to be an SVC), the two verbs establish a purposive relationship. The basic form of SVCs with shared objects is [NP₁ V₁ NP₂ V₂(NP₂).]

(105) T*a*   ***zhong***   cai   mai.

　　　 S/he   **plant**   vegetable **sell**

　　　 'S/he planted vegetables to sell. '

(106) T*a*   ***jie***   qian   yong.

　　　 S/he   **borrow**   money   **use**

　　　 'She borrowed money to spend. '

Chinese is classified as an SVO language. Normally a sentence should contain a subject followed by a verb. If a verb is transitive it should be followed by an object. In examples (105) and (106), the first three words form the canonical structure SVO. However, for the second verbs *mai* 'sell' in (105) and *yong* 'use' in (106), even though these verbs are transitive, there are no NPs preceding or following them to serve as their logical subjects or objects. Then how can it happen that the second verb has no object although it is transitive? Baker (1989) and Liu (1991) claim that the second verb in this construction discharges an internal theta role (theme) to its previous NP, resulting in a shared object in addition to a shared subject. In fact, in this kind of construction, there is an implied subject and an implied object. Sharing both a subject and an object in this construction suggests a tighter relationship between two VPs.

5.4.1 *The Three Principles Reflected in Double-headed Constructions*

In a double-headed SVC we find that the objects of the embedded or downstairs verbs are typically missing even though these verbs may be transitive. However, the absence of a direct object following the second verb does not affect its status as a transitive verb because it shares its theme arguments with the matrix verb. On the other hand, if we put an overt object after the second verb the resulting sentences would be either ungrammatical or change the meaning of the sentence. Consider these versions of (107) and (108):

(107) # * *Ta* **zhong** *cai*　　**mai**　*cai.*

　　　　S/he **plant** vegetable **sell** vegetable.

(108) # * *Ta* **jie**　　*qian*　**yong** *qian.*

　　　　S/he **borrow** money **use**　money.

The ungrammaticality of sentences (107) and (108) shows that the omission of an object for the second verb in this kind of SVC is by no means optional, but obligatory. How can we account for the phenomenon that V_1 and V_2 have to share a subject but also an object in this kind of construction?

The fact that the second set of arguments are omitted suggests to the speaker/hearer that they are identical to the arguments in the first clause and so this further suggests a very tight conceptual connection, hence an interpretation as an SVC. There exists a relationship of situational interdependence between the two verbs in this kind of SVC. The first event serves as the means for the second event or the first event is conducted for the purpose of enabling the execution of the second event. In (107), the purpose of *zhong cai* 'plant vegetables' is *mai cai* 'sell vegetables'; if the subject does not plant vegetables he has no vegetables to sell. In (108) *jie qian* 'borrow money' serves as the means to get money to spend; if the subject doesn't borrow money it is likely that he has no money to spend. So constructions with both a shared subject and a shared object are actually like "tighter" purposive clauses.

The dependence of the two verbs is also reflected in their temporal sequence. In this type of SVC the first action must precede the second chronologically. When two dependent verbs bear a relation of temporal or causal sequence they may share an entity, which results in an object shared by two verbs in SVCs. In the case of SVCs, the obligatorily shared object provides a means to link the two verbs closely to reflect a sense of semantic dependence between them.

5.4.2 *Schematic Representation*

To serve as backgrounds for the schematic representation for clausal complement constructions, first I would like to pictorially represent an event based on a Langecher-style notation. A canonical transitive event (e. g. 'He pressed the button.') featuring a relation ($\longrightarrow$) between two event participants ($\textcircled{P}$) can be represented as the following figure:

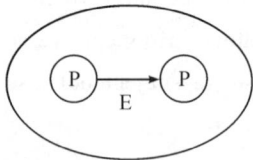

Figure 5.4   A canonical transitive event

A transitive event with an omitted but implied object (e. g. ' She ate. ') can be presented in Figure 5.5:

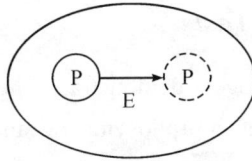

Figure 5.5   A transitive event with an omitted but implied object

With the above two figures serving as backgrounds, the schematic representation of SVCs with double-headed constructions can be illustrated in Figure 5.6:

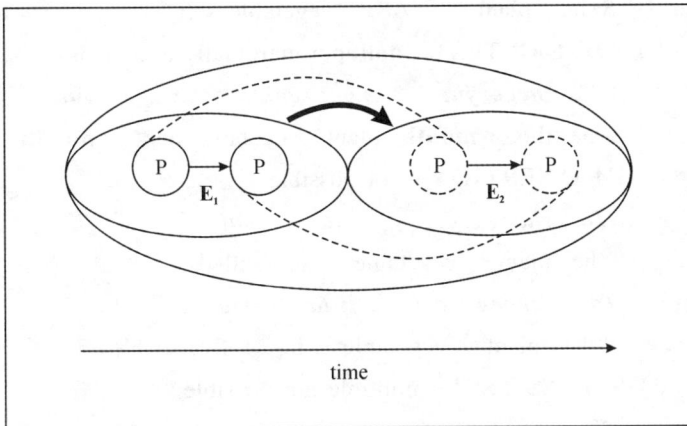

Figure 5.6   A construction with both a shared subject
and a shared object

Figure 5.6 illustrates a double-headed construction. The heavy arrow between $EVENT_1$ and $EVENT_2$ indicates that the two events are causally linked. The big oval encompassing two smaller ovals suggests that $EVENT_1$ and $EVENT_2$ conceptually comprise one unifying event. The dashed lines linking the two circles which represent participants indicate that both a subject and an object in $EVENT_1$ are identical with those in $event_2$ respectively. The two circles in dashed lines in $EVENT_2$ suggest that the two participants are covert or omitted, which leads to a construction with a shared subject and a shared object as well.

5.4.3 *Application of Tests*

The following sentences demonstrate the application to double-headed constructions of the morphosyntactic and prosodic tests proposed in this study for determining SVC status:

(109) (a) **LE TEST**—2 not possible

<blockquote>

* *Ta*   *zhong*   *le*   *cai*   *mai*   *le.*

   S/he   plant   **ASP**   vegetable sell   **ASP**
</blockquote>

(a') *Ta*   *zhong*   *le*   *cai*   *mai.*

   S/he   plant   **ASP**   vegetable sell

(b) **ADVERB TEST**—multiple marginally acceptable

? *Ta* ***zhege yue***   *zhong cai*   ***xiage***   ***yue***   *mai.*

   S/he **this**   **month**   plant   vegetable **next**   **month** sell

(c) **TA INSERTION**—not possible

* *Ta*   *zhong*   *cai*   ***ta***   *mai.*

   S/he   plant   vegetable s/**he**   sell

(c') *Ta*   *zhong*   *cai*   ***ta***   *mai cai.*

   S/he   plant   vegetable s/**he**   sellvegetable

(d) **STRESS TEST**—multiple not possible

* *Ta*   *'zhong*   *cai*   *'mai.*

   S/he   **plant**   vegetable **sell**

(e) **REVERSIBILITY TEST**—irreversible

* *Ta*   ***mai***   *cai*   ***zhong.***

   S/he   **sell**   vegetable **plant**

(f) **BA TEST**—2 not possible

Ta   ***ba***   *cai*   *zhong*   *le*   *mai.*

   S/he **OBJ**   vegetable plant   ASP   sell

(g) **PAUSE TEST**—pause not possible

* *Ta*   *zhang*   *cai,*   (...)   *mai.*

S/he plant vegetable,   sell

Double-headed constructions generally allow one *le* to be attached to the matrix verb as shown in (109a′) and one temporal averb specification. If *ta* is restored between the two VPs the object cannot be shared between them as shown in (109c′) and in that case, the resulting sentences are best considered as an instance of coordination. They receive one main stress on the entire verb complex as shown in (109d). The *ba* test shows that one *ba* construction is possible in this structure as shown in (109f). A pause occurring between two VPs is infelicitous.

5.4.4 Discussion

When multiple temporal adverb specifications occur in a double-headed construction, the resulting sentence is at best marginally acceptable. If two temporal adverb specifications are needed in this structure usually the sentence should be re-written with the second event coded as a relative clause:

(110) *Ta   zhege   yue   zhong de   cai   xiage   yue   mai.*
S/he this   month plant **RC** vegetable next   month sell
'Next month he will sell the vegetables which he planted this month. '

The morphosyntactic and prosodic tests proposed in this study show that sentences with double-headed constructions like example (4) basically manifest the properties of one unifying conceptual event with multiple micro phases. Thus, they can be classified as real SVCs.

The binding force between the two verb phrases in this type of SVC is relatively strong, that is, stronger than that in the type of SVC with two discrete events in which one serves as the purposive complement of the other, but not as strong as that in the type of SVC with VV compounds in which one verb is completely incorporated into another. As I have argued, double-headed constructions should be construed as strictly abiding by the Principle of Temporal Sequence. A relatively greater force binding the two sequenced verbs together through obligatorily sharing the same reference as objects suggests a relatively higher sense of dependence between them.

5.5 The So-called VV Compounds—A Continuum Between Lexicon and Syntax

Whether Chinese VV compounds are lexicalized units or derived syntactically has been a long-time debate among Chinese linguists. Traditional analyses assume that Chinese VV compounds are either in the realm of lexicon or syntactic phenomena but are not both. This study proposes that Chinese VV compounds are not a discrete category. Cognitive Grammar (Langacker 1987, 1991) holds that lexicon and syntax form a continuum. In fact, Chinese VV compounds display a continuum between lexicon and syntax. Some so-called VV compounds are best analyzed as lexicalized items while others are really serial verb constructions (e. g. Paul 2004).

5.5.1 Parallel VV Compounds

In the VV compound category, some items are simply fixed lexicalized units. These compounds are mostly parallel VV compounds. Li and Thompson (1981: 68) claim that "the vast majority of parallel verb compounds have developed as the Mandarin language, which once contained a predominance of monosyllabic words, has gained an ever-increasing number of polysyllabic words." For example, the concept 'fortunate' was expressed by the monosyllabic word *xing* 'fortunate' at an earlier stage of Mandarin Chinese; however, in Modern Mandarin, this concept is expressed by the parallel compound *xing-fu* 'fortunate-blessed— fortunate' (Li & Thompson 1981).

In some parallel VV compounds two verbs either are synonymous or signal the same type of predicative notions (Li & Thompson, 1981). The constituents of these verb compounds are of the same syntactic category. For example, if the constituents are transitive verbs, the compound is also a transitive verb such as *ti-huan* ' replace-change—replace '. The followings are examples of two basic kinds of parallel verb compounds (Li & Thompson 1981) :

(i) V1 and V2 are synonyms or near synonyms :

(111) *gou-mai* ' purchase-buy—buy '

　　　qing-zhu ' celebrate-bless—celebrate '

　　　bang-zhu ' help-assist—help '

　　　jian-cha ' check-examine— examine '

　　　zhi-liao ' treat-cure—cure '

　　　chong-bai ' respect-worship— worship '

(ii) V1 and V2 are similar in meaning :

(112) *piao-liu* ' drift-flow—drift '

　　　fu-yang ' support-care for—raise '

　　　fang-qi ' loosen-abandon—give up '

　　　ti-huan ' replace-change—replace '

　　　fen-san ' separate-disperse—separate and disperse '

　　In Mandarin Chinese, there are some parallel VV compounds whose meanings are not directly or only partially related to those of their components such as *chu ru* ' exit enter—(have) differences ', and *li kai* ' separate-open—leave '. Such compounds abide by Lexical Integrity Principle (Huang 1984) and nothing can intervene between their two constituents. For example, the perfective aspect marker *le* can not occur between the constituents of these compounds. For these somewhat opaque compounds, their compositional value may not remain a significant factor in their meanings and it is better to list them in the lexicon as fixed units.

5.5.2 *Phase VV Compounds*

　　Different from opaque VV compounds, most VV compounds in Mandarin Chinese are quite transparent semantically and each of their constituents can be used freely as a word on its own. These transparent VV compounds can be classified into three groups—phase, resultative and directional compounds, which display various degrees of syntactic properties. In phase compounds, the second verb constituent indicates the phase of the first verb. Li and Thompson (1981: 65) claim that in phase VV compounds "the second part denotes something more like the type of action described by the first verb or the degree to which it is carried out than its result". The following are different types of common phase VV compounds, which are grouped together according to the second constituent expressing the phase of the action in the first verb (Li & Thompson 1981).

(i) wan ' finish', which signals the completion of an action

(113) *xie wan* ' write-finish — finish writing'

　　　duo wan ' read-finish — finish reading'

　　　zuo wan ' do-finish — finish doing'

　　　chang wan ' sing-finish — finish singing'

　　　xue wan ' study-finish — finish studying'

　　　nong wan ' do-finish — finish doing'

(ii) zhao ' be on target':

(114) *zhao zhao* ' search-be on target — find'

　　　shuo zhao ' say-be on target — say (it) right'

　　　cai zhao ' guess-be on target — guess right'

　　　yong zhao ' use-be on target — get to use'

(iii) zhu ' hold on'

(115) *zhan zhu* ' stand-hold on — stand still'

　　　ting zhu ' stop-hold on — stop firmly'

　　　zhua zhu ' grab-hold on — grab onto'

　　　guan zhu ' control-hold on — control'

　　　liu zhu ' keep-hold on — keep or detain'

　　In phase VV compounds, *bu* ' not' or *de* ' achievable' can be usually inserted between these compounds to indicate that the result can be obtained or cannot be achieved as (116) and (117) show.

(116) *Ta   chi   de   wan   yu.*

     3SG   eat   DE   finish   fish

     'S/he can finish eating the fish. '

(117) *Ta   chi   bu   wan   yu.*

     3SG   eat   not   finish   fish

     'S/he cannot finish eating the fish. '

In phase VV compounds, except *bu* 'not' or *de* 'achievable' nothing else can intervene between the constituents. For example, the perfective aspect marker *le* cannot occur between two constituents of phase compounds as (118) illustrates.

(118) *＊ Ta   chi   le   wan   yu.*

     3SG   eat   PERF   finish   fish

5.5.3 *Resultative VV Compounds*

In Mandarin Chinese, the need for resultative complements is due to the fact that many Mandarin action verbs only convey the meaning of the action phase but not the result phase (e. g. Talmy 2000). Thus, such action verbs often require other verbs as complements to specify realization or fulfillment. The example in (119) is entirely acceptable in Chinese but sounds strange in English:

(119) *Wo   sha   le   zhu (keshi   mei sha   si).*

     I   kill   PERF   pig (but   NEG kill die)

     ＊'I killed the pig but it didn't die. '

(120) *Wo   sha   si   le   zhu.*

     I   kill   die   PERF pig

     'I killed the pig. '

The semantics of the examples in (119) and (120) can be explained as follows. In (119), the first clause means that the speaker performed the action with the intention of killing the pig and the second clause in parentheses indicates that the action did not achieve the goal, i. e. success in killing the pig. In contrast, with the confirmational satellite *si* 'die' in (120), the sentence is now an undeniable assertion that the speaker succeeded in killing the pig.

Thus, the English verb *kill* used to gloss the Chinese verb *sha* does not correspond fully in meaning. Therefore, a sentence gloss like 'I killed the pig but the pig didn't die' is really contradictory in English and thus, incorrectly represents the non-paradoxical Mandarin Chinese original. The original meaning is that 'I performed the action with the intent to kill, but the pig didn't die.' English verbs such as kill, open, kick are generally construed to refer to a simplex action of the fulfillment type and they specify the attainment of a certain final state (Talmy 1985, 2000; Yin 2008).

In Mandarin Chinese, the concept covered by a typical English verb such as *kill* is divided into two parts: the final outcome, usually conformed by a verb complement and an action performed with the intent to lead to that outcome, which is signaled by the main verb. As a result, the unitary concept of an English verb often has a counterpart in Mandarin Chinese with two-part conceptualization expressed by a verb plus another verb to indicate result.

Therefore, in Mandarin Chinese, unlike in English, some action verbs often do not specify the results by themselves. It is often verbal complements in the V2 position that specify the result-state. One of the most frequent resultative complements is *dao*. With *dao* being used together with action verbs, the results of the action verbs are signaled. For example, when *ting* 'listen' is used with *dao* 'reach, get to', the resulting construction is interpreted as 'hear something' (the result of the action of listening has been achieved).

Another good example to illustrate that Mandarin speakers often add another verbal morpheme to an action-only verb to indicate the result would be *kan* 'look' vs. *kan-jian* 'look-perceive—see'. A verb like *kan* 'direct one's gaze, look' only encodes the meaning of looking, without indicating whether the looking has led to perception or not. When Mandarin speakers want to convey the meaning that not only the action has taken place but also results have been achieved, they need to add resultative verbal complements. Thus, when Mandarin speakers want to express the meaning equivalent to English ' see ' they need to use two verbal morphemes: one is *kan* ' look ' and the other is *jian* ' perceive '. In the case of English, a different strategy for conveying the result meaning of verbs is used. It does not add resultative complements to action-only verbs but uses entirely new verbs, which include both the action-phase and the result-phase as in *look* vs. *see*.

Like phase VV compounds, resultative VV compounds allow the insertion of *bu* ' not ' or *de* ' achievable ' between their constituents as (121) and (122) indicate.

(121) *Ta   kan   de   dao   feiji.*

　　　3SG   look   DE   reach, achieve plane

　　　' S/he can see the plane. '

(122) *Ta   kan   bu   dao   feiji.*

　　　3SG   look   NEG   reach, achieve plane

　　　' S/he cannot see the plane. '

Moreover, in some resultative VV compounds, certain adverbs such as *quan* ' completely ' can insert between the constituents to indicate degrees as (123) shows.

(123) *Beizi   da   de   quan   sui   le.*

　　　cup   hit   DE   completely   break   PERF

　　　' The cup was hit completely broken to pieces '.

5.5.4 *Directional VV Compounds*

Directional verb compounds are another type of semantically transparent VV compound. Motion verbs are very frequently used as V2 to indicate direction to form directional compounds (e. g. , Li & Thompson 1981; Zou 1994). This type of compound has the schematic nature ［V1MOTION/ACTION V2DIRECTION］, in which the second verb signifies the path or direction of the first verb, as illustrated in (124) and (125). In these two examples, the verbs in the V2 position do not specify motion in their own right, but only the direction or the path of the motion or action suggested by the first verb, the main verb.

(124) *Zhangshan   da   bu   zou   lai.*

   Zhangshan   big   step   walk come

   'Zhangshan walked over here in big steps.'

(125) *Lisi xiang   tingche   chu   zou   qu.*

   Lisi toward   parking   place walk go

   'Lisi walked away toward the parking lot.'

In directional compounds, the second verb, typically one of the motion verbs *lai* 'come' or *qu* 'go', indicates the direction of the first verb. In Mandarin Chinese, certain verbs, typically verbs of displacement, show up as the first verb in directional compounds. As Li and Thompson (1981) have observed, the most obvious type of displacement verb is a verb of motion such as *pao* 'run', *zou* 'walk', fei 'fly', *gun* 'roll'. Another common type of displacement verb is a dislocation verb, a verb that "inherently implies that the direct object undergoes a change of location" (Li & Thompson 1981: 58) such as *ban* 'remove', *reng* 'throw', *song* 'send', *ji* 'mail', *ju* 'lift', *fang* 'put', *duan* 'carry'. These verbs generally conflate movement with some other activity.

Prototypically, the second verbs in directional compounds are *lai* 'come' and *qu* 'go', although there is a small set of additional verbs which function as complements of direction. The verbs *lai* 'come' and *qu* 'go' are used extensively in Mandarin compounds as complements of direction. They occur after verbs of movement or action to indicate direction 'towards' or 'away from' a preferred deictic centre as in (126) (Yip & Don 1998).

(126) a. *Ta   na   lai   le   yi   ping   jiu.*

3SG   carry   come   PERF one   CL   wine

'S/he brought a bottle of wine. '

b. *Ta   na   qu   le   yi ping jiu.*

3SG   carry   go   PERF one CL   wine

'S/he took a bottle of wine with him. '

Besides *lai* and *qu*, there is a small group of Mandarin motion verbs (e. g. *jin* 'enter', *chu* 'exit', *qi* 'rise', *hui* 'return', *guo* 'cross', *kai* 'open') which also participate in directional compounds (Li & Thompson 1981, Lamarre 2007, Lin 2001, Xiao & McEnery 2004). These verbs are mainly used in directional complements to express directional meanings and they are seldom used as independent verbs (Li & Thompson 1981). Two examples are given below:

(127) *Ta   zuo jin   le   shangdian.*

3SG   walk enter   PERF   store.

'S/he walked into the store. '

(128) *Ta   fang   hui   le   liang ben   shu.*

3SG   put   return PERF two   CL   book

'S/he put two books back. '

In directional VV compounds, it is also possible to insert *bu* 'not' or *de* 'achievable' between their constituents as (129) and (130) indicate.

(129) a. *Ta   na   de   lai   yi   xiang   shu.*

3SG   carry   DE   come   one   CL   book

'S/hecan bring a box of books here. '

b. *Ta   na   bu   lai   yi   xiang   shu.*

3SG   carry   NEG   come   one   CL   book

'S/hecannot bring a box of books here. '

(130) a. *Ta   ban   de   qu   yi   xiang   shu.*

3SG move   DE   go   one CL   book

'S/hecan take a box of books away. '

b. *Ta   ban   bu   qu   yi   xiang   shu.*

3SG move NEGgo   one CL   book

' S/he cannot take a box of books away. '

In addition to allowing the insertion of *bu* ' not ' or *de* ' achievable ' between their constituents, this type of compound also permits the perfective aspect marker *le* to intervene between the two constituents as (131) shows.

(131) a. *Ta   ba   yi   ben   shu   na   le   lai   le.*

3SG   OGJ one CL   book   carry PERF come   PERF

' S/he brought a book (here). '

b. *Ta   ba   yi   ben   shu   na   le   qu   le.*

3SG   OBJ one CL   book carry   PERF go   PERF

' S/he took a book away. '

Moreover, in the so-called directional compounds, it is possible for their objects to occur between the first constituent and the directional complement as (132) illustrates.

ᵤ (132) a. *Ta   na   le   yi   ben   shu   lai.*

3SG   carry   PERF one CL   book come

' S/he brought a book (here). '

b. *Ta   na   le   yi   ben   shu   qu.*

3SG   carry   PERF one CL   book go

' S/he took a book away. '

Directional VV compounds do not lose their internal grammatical structure or cease to instantiate schematic constructions. Their compositional value remains a significant factor in their meanings. Therefore, those compounds could be viewed as being formed by the assembling of their components and could be regarded as highly integrated serial verb constructions.

To sum up, the so-called VV compounds in Mandarin Chinese are not a discrete or homogenous category, but display a graded phenomenon. Cognitive Grammar holds that lexicon and syntax form a continuum and Mandarin Chinese VV compounds actually display some properties between lexicon and syntax. Parallel VV compounds are typical lexicalized compounds and phase VV compounds display more properties as lexical items rather than as syntactic constructions. However, resultative VV compounds display more characteristics as syntactic compounds and directional VV compounds show typical syntactic properties. Therefore, it is reasonable to analyze resultative VV compounds and directional VV compounds as serial verb constructions. Thus, in this study, VV compounds treated as SVCs include resultative and directional VV compounds.

In terms of Mandarin Chinese VV compounds, the continuum between lexicon and syntax is the following: parallel VV compounds > > phase VV compounds > > resultative VV compounds > > directional VV compounds.

5.6 *VV Compounds as SVCs*

An SVC made up of a VV compound refers to structures in which one or more verbs serve as the complement(s) of a head verb. The two verbs in this type of SVC display an absolute degree of interdependence. They are very closely linked to each other and seem to coalesce such that they are no longer really interpretable as two discrete events in the case of a VV sequence, but as a new verbal complex whereby they express one conceptual event with two phases. They are so dependent on each other that on many occasions they are morphologically bound and we can best analyze them as a VV compound. This type of structure reflects the extreme case of serialization and it should be placed on the far end of the interdependence continuum given in Figure 4. 1. There are two major kinds of complements in VV compounds: resultative complements and directional complements.

5.6.1 SVCs with Complements of Result

In Mandarin Chinese, complements of result in VV compounds are cases in which the second verb indicates a result of the action of the first verb. Verbs used as complements of result are very restricted lexically. The commonly used ones are the following phase verbs or achievement verbs: *po* ' break ', *dao* ' fall ', *diao* ' drop ', *kai* ' open, separate ', *wan* ' finish ', *dao* ' attain, achieve '. These verbs serving as complements express the phases or achievements of the first verbs (head verbs). In English, the resulting state is usually indicated by an adjective or prepositional particle—in short, by an atemporal relational predication (Langacker, 1987), while in Chinese, the resulting state is often indicated by a complement verb or adjective which usually follows the head verb immediately.

(133) a. *Ta   tui   dao   le   wo.*

    S/he **push** **fall** ASP I

    ' S/he pushed me down. '

    b. *Ta   dao   tui   le   wo.*

    S/he **fall** **push** ASPI

(134) *Zhangsan   muo   qu   le   zang   dongxi.*

    Zhangsan **wipe** **go** ASP dirty   thing

    ' Zhangsan wiped the dirty things away. '

(135) *Lisi   la   kai   le   men.*

    Lisi **pull open** ASP door

    ' Lisi pulled the door open. '

In (133a) the result of pushing is that the things being pushed *fall*; in (134) the result of wiping the dirty things is that the dirty things are *gone* and in (135) the result of pulling the door is that the door finally *opens*.

In this type of structure, like other types of SVCs, the order of the two verbs cannot be reversed, otherwise ungrammatical sentences would result as in (133b). V_2 can even be regarded as a bound particle of V_1

and virtually nothing can be inserted between the two verbs except the two infixes (Li & Thompson, 1981) *de* ' can or achievable ' and *bu* ' cannot or unachievable ' , which will be discussed shortly. Even if the object is logically shared as a participant by both V_1 and V_2, this object can only be put after V_2 rather thanput between them, nor can it be repeated, as the following examples illustrate:

(136) a. ** Ta   tui   **wo**   dao   le.*

S/he   push   I   fall   ASP

' S/he pushed me down. '

b. ** Ta   tui   **wo**   dao   **wo**   le.*

S/he   push   I   fall   I   ASP

' S/he pushed me down. '

In (136), the VV sequence is regarded as one verbal complex and, accordingly, the object *wo* ' me ' should be put at the end of this complex; otherwise, ungrammatical sentences will result.

The aspectual participle *le* in Chinese is normally placed after verbs to indicate aspect. However, it cannot be inserted between the two compounded verbs. Rather, it must be placed after the two verbs. This indicates that the two verbs constitute a VV compound and that they form a conceptually single unit.

(137) ** Ta   tui   **le**   dao   wo.*

S/he   push   ASP   fall   I

One important characteristic of SVCs with complements of result is that they can occur in the potential form. The potential form involves the insertion of *de* ' obtainable ' or *bu* ' not ' between the VV string. " The insertion of *de* has the effect of giving the compound an affirmative meaning, ' can ' , whereas the insertion of *bu* gives the compound a negative meaning, ' cannot ' " (Li & Thompson, 1981: 56) as the following examples illustrate:

(138) a. *Ta   tui   **de**   dao   wo.*

S/he   push   obtainable   fall   me

'S/he can push me down. '

'S/he can push me and achieve my falling down. '

  b. *Ta   tui **bu** dao   wo.*

     S/he push not fall   me

     'S/he cannot push me down. '

(139) a. *Zhangsan muo **de**   diao zang dongxi.*

      Zhangsan wipe obtain   drop dirty thing

      'Zhangsan can wipe the dirty things away. '

  b. *Zhangsan muo **bu** diao zang dongxi.*

     Zhangsan wipe not drop dirty thing

     'Zhangsan cannot wipe the dirty things away. '

Li and Thompson (1981) have observed that the English translations of the constructions exemplified in (138) - (139) above with the auxiliary verbs 'can' or 'cannot' do not completely convey the meanings of the potential forms in Mandarin Chinese. The presence of the infix *de* in these examples means that the action or process denoted by V_1 of the compound can achieve the result denoted by V_2 of the compound. The presence of the negative infix signals that the action cannot achieve the result. The glosses 'can' and 'cannot' are used in (138) and (139); however, it would perhaps be better to express the meanings as 'achievable' or 'unachievable'. Therefore, (a) means 's/he pushes me and can achieve my falling' while (b) means that 's/he pushes me but fails to achieve my falling'.

The possibility of infixation by *de* or *bu* between the first constituent and the second constituent of such compounds indicates that the second constituent still displays properties of verbs. Accordingly, the second constituent of these compounds can best be analyzed as a verb rather than as a preposition or adjective as in the English glosses.

When the emphasis is to be put on the cause-effect relation between the two VPs, a conjunction such as *suoyi* 'therefore' can be inserted to indicate such a relationship, as the following example shows:

(140) *Ta   tui   wo   **shuyi**   wo   dao xia   le.*

S/he push   me   **therefore** me   fall   descent ASP

'S/he pushed me and therefore I fell down. '

Now the two verbs occur in two separate clauses as independent main verbs as in (140). This is additional evidence to show that the second constituents in such VV compounds display the properties of verbs rather than prepositions.

In Mandarin, action verbs like *tui* 'push', *da* 'beat' and *ti* 'kick' can be modified by a quantifier or an adverb of intensity while compounds like *ti dao* 'kick fall' cannot have a quantifier or an adverb to intervene its constituents.

(141) a. *Ta   ti   le   wo   **liang   xia**.*

S/he   kick   ASP   me   **two   time**

'S/he kicked me twice. '

b. ** Ta   ti   le   **liang   xia**   dao   wo.*

S/he   kick ASP **two   time**   fall   me

(142) a. *Ta   **shijin**   ti   wo.*

S/he **fiercely**   kick   me

'S/he fiercely kicked. '

b. ** Ta   **shijin**   ti   dao   wo.*

S/he   **fiercely** kick fall   me

When these action verbs are used alone they can be modified by a quantifier or an adverb of intensity. However, when they are used in compounds, they seem to lose such properties. How should we account for this? The answer lies in the fact that V_1 and V_2 in such compounds are bound together to form a single unit and thus express a single conceptual event. They display the characteristics of a combination of the two verbs rather than those of two individual verbs respectively because these "separate verbs do not denote individuated events" (Frawley, 1992: 143). As stated previously, this kind of SVC comprised of VV compounds exemplifies the highest degree of verb serialization or near coalescence in Mandarin Chinese.

One of the remarkable characteristics of these compound verbs is that they are often actions and thus they generally signal a high degree of transitivity. Action verbs rank high on Hopper and Thompson's transitivity scale (Hopper and Thompson, 1980). Usually only verbs with a relatively high degree of transitivity can be used in *ba* structures. Therefore, the *ba* construction has been regarded as a highly transitive type of clause (Ji, 1997). As a result, *ba* structures [S *ba*-(object marker) O V] can be used to prepose their shared objects of VV compounds of action.

(143) *Lisi* **ba** men la-kai-le.

     Lisi **BA** door pull-open-ASP

     'Lisi pulled the door open. '

If verb compounds do not signal a relatively high sense of transitivity, other means such as appropriate discourse contextualization should be employed to increase its transitivity or sense of action (or movement) in order to be eligible for the use of *ba* structures. "The creation of the appropriate context in fact involves an interplay of various kinds of transitivizing factors" (ibid. 1997: 11). Another way to increase an event's transitivity profile is to add some words which "generally serve to make the *ba* sentence perfective or specify a conceptual boundary of the event" (ibid. 1997:12) since the *ba* construction requires its verb to be bounded.

(144) a. *Zhangsan xiang-qi-le*   *zhuyi.*

       Zhangsan think-rise-ASP   idea

       'Zhangsan came cross an idea. '

       'An idea occurred to Zhangsan. '

    b. *Zhangsan* **ba** *zhuyi xiang-qi-**lai**-le.*

       Zhangsan **BA** idea   think-rise-come-ASP

       'Zhangsan thought out an idea. '

In (144b), the verb *lai* 'come' is added to the VV compound in order to increase the sense of movement to make it more dynamic since the verb *xiang* 'think' does not signal a very high sense of transitivity. On the other hand, the verb *xiangqi* 'think-rise, occur to' seems to be unbounded and the attachment of *lai* 'come' to this VV compound gives *xiangqi* an endpoint, and thus specifying a conceptual boundary to the event, which also increases its transitivity. As a result, with the addition of *lai* to the VV compound *xiangqi* the overall event can be made to fit in with *ba* constructions to prepose the object. This example also illustrates the metaphorical use of the verbs as complements: *qi* 'rise' and *lai* 'come' indicate the result of mental activity. An idea is coming or arising as the result of Zhangsan's thinking process.

5.6.2 SVCs with Complements of Direction

In Chinese, certain verbs, typically verbs of displacement, can serve as directional complements of the main verbs (V_1). As Li and Thompson (1981) have observed, the most obvious type of displacement verb is a verb of motion such as *pao* 'run', *zou* 'walk', *fei* 'fly' *gun* 'roll'. Another common type of displacement verb is a dislocation verb "that inherently implies that the direct object undergoes a change of location" (Li & Thompson, 1981:58) such as *ban* 'remove', *reng* 'throw', *song* 'send', *ji* 'mail', *ju* 'lift', *fang* 'put', *duan* 'carry'. These verbs conflate movement with some other activity. As for V_2 denoting direction, they are highly limited lexically. The prototypical ones are *lai* 'come' and *qu* 'go', although there is a small set of additional verbs which function as complements of direction. I'll discuss these in turn.

5.6.2.1 *SVCs with Verbs* lai '*come*' *and* qu '*go*' *as Complements*

The verbs *lai* 'come' and *qu* 'go' are used extensively in Mandarin SVCs as complements of direction. They occur after verbs of movement or action to indicate a direction 'towards' or 'away from' the speaker (Yip & Don, 1998a). Typically, these involve events of TRANSPORTATION as in (145) or TRANSACTION (TRANSLOCATION) as in (146):

(145) a. *Zhangsan*　　**pao**　　**lai**-*le*.

　　　　Zhangsan　　**run**　　come-ASP

　　　　'Zhangsan run over here. '

　　b. *Lisi*　　**pao**　　**qu**-*le*.

　　　Lisi　　**run**　　**go**- ASP

　　　'Lisi run over there. '

(146) a. *Zhangsan*　**na**　　**lai**-*le*　　　*yiben*　　*shu*.

　　　　Zhangsan　**carry**　**come**- ASP　one-CL　　book

　　　　'Zhangsan brought a book. '

　　b. *Lisi*　**na**　　**qu**-*le*　　　*yiben*　　*shu*.

　　　Lisi　**carry**　**go**- ASP　　　one-CL　　book

　　　'Lisi took a book with him. '

The verbs in these sentences are bound together and the verb of movement is naturally accompanied by direction. Generally they are inseparable as shown in (147):

(147) **Lisi*　*na*　　　**xingqier**　*qu-le*　　　*yiben*　　*shu*.

　　　Lisi　　carry　**Tuesday**　go-ASP　one-CL　　book

Furthermore, if there is only one perfective aspect particle *le* used in a sentence, it can only be attached to the end of the verbal complex rather than put between the two verbs:

(148) **Zhangsan*　*pao-le*　　　*lai*.

　　　　Zhangsan　　run-**ASP**　　come

(149) **Lisi*　*na-le*　　　*qu*　*yiben*　　*shu*.

　　　Lisi　　carry-**ASP**　go　one-CL　　book

5.6.2.2 *Double Complements and their Figurative Uses*

There is a small group of motion verbs in Mandarin other than *lai* and *qu* which also participate in VV compounds. These verbs have directional meanings when they occur as directional complements in addition to verbal meanings when they are used as independent verbs (Li

& Thompson, 1981). Two examples are given below:

(150) *Ta   zuo   jin   le   jiaoshi.*

S/he **walk   enter** ASP classroom.

'S/he walked into the classroom. '

(151) *Ta   fang   xia   le   shubao.*

S/he **put   descend** ASP schoolbag

'S/he laid down her/his schoolbag. '

There are about eight verbs in this group (ibid.): *shang* 'ascend',
xia 'descend', *jin* 'enter', *chu* 'exit', *qi* 'rise', *hui* 'return', *guo*
'cross', *kai* 'open'. *Lai* 'come' and *qu* 'go' may be linked to the
group of 8 motion verbs (Yip & Don, 1998b) in Chinese to form a set of
double directional complements elaborating some movement or action.
Therefore, there are 16 members in this category of double complements
when the 8 verbs combine with *lai* and *qu*.

A. following verbs of movement (absolute motion)

(152) *Huar   diao   xia-lai-le.*

Picture **drop descend-come**-ASP

'The picture fell down. '

(153) *Che   kai   guo-qu-le.*

Car   **drive   cross-go**-ASP

'The car went past. '

B. following verbs of action (translocation)

(154) *Shu   fang   hui-qu-le.*

Book **put   return-go**-ASP

'The book was put back. '

(155) *Cai   duan   jin-lai-le.*

Dish **bring   enter-come**- ASP

'The dishes were brought in. '

These double complements display properties of being construable as a
single conceptual unit. For example, the particle *le* cannot be preposed
from the post-compound position to a position between the VVV

compounds as the following examples show:

(156) * Shu   fang   **le**   hui-qu.

       Book   put   **ASP**   return-go

       'The bowl has been put in place. '

(157) * Cai   duan   **le**   jin-lai.

       Dish   bring   **ASP**   enter-come

       'The dish has been brought in. '

Sometimes these double complements can have metaphorical interpretations in appropriate contexts besides being used literally as in (158). In that case, the VV compounds could be regarded as having been lexicalized.

(158) Ni   yinggai   ti   ta   **shang-lai**.

       You   should   pick   him   **ascend-come**

       'You should lift him up. '

       'You should promote him. '

Here *shanglai* 'ascend-come' can be used figuratively: come up high in social (or administrative) position and the metaphorical meaning is derived from the basic meaning *shanglai* 'come up'.

(159) Ta   xiang   huo   **xia-qu**.

       S/he   want   live   **descend-go**

       'He wants to live on. '

In (159) *xia-qu* is also used figuratively. The directional aspect of *xia-qu* is metaphorically extended to the aspect of time (Li & Thompson, 1981). Therefore, *huo xia-qu* 'live descend-go' is interpreted as 'live on'. The double compound *xia qu* has lexicalized.

5.6.2.3 *The Behaviors of Directional Complements*

Compounds with directional complements behave like those with resultative complements to a large extent. When used independently, motion verbs like *pao* 'run' can be modified by a quantifier while a quantifier cannot modify a motion verb when it is in a compound like *pao lai* ' run come ' .

(160) a. *Ta   pao   le   **san**   **ci**.*

S/he   run   ASP   **three**   **time**

' S/he has run three times. '

* b. *Ta   pao   le   **san**   **ci**   lai.*

S/he   run   ASP   **three**   **time**   come

' S/he has run here three times. '

In the same vein, it is natural to modify an action verb like *zhua* ' catch ' while it is not quite natural to modify an action verb in a compound with a directional complement.

(161) a. *Ta   **shijin**   zhua   dongxi.*

S/he   **fiercely**   hold (catch)   thing

' S/he fiercely caught things (or something) . '

? b. *Ta   **shijin**   zhua   lai   le   dongxi.*

S/he   **fiercely**   hold (catch) come   ASP   thing

Therefore, compounds with directional complements display the characteristics of extreme coalescence or serialization to the point of losing their basic lexical senses. In other words, two verbs in such constructions behave like a novel verb complex rather than as two individual verbs. They are often bound together and in most cases lexicalized to form a single unit and thus express a single conceptual action or event.

In SVCs with $V_2(V_3)$ as complements, $V_1 V_2(V_3)$ have a referent to share, either the subject or both the subject and the object if both V_1 and V_2 are transitive. These verbs are so dependent on each other that normally they are bound together to form a verb compound. They must abide by the iconicity principle of temporal sequence or scope. The constructions with verbs as complements (both resultative ones and directional ones) that we have analyzed here meet all the three principles proposed in this study.

5.6.3 *Schematic Representation*

The schematic representation of SVCs with VV compounds can be illustrated in Figure 5.7:

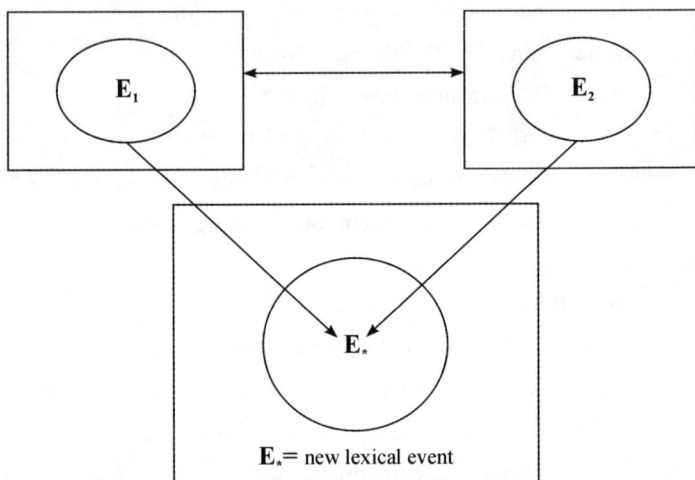

E_*= new lexical event

Figure 5.7   Illustration of total event conflation and highest degree of VV serialization

Figure 5.7 displays the limiting case of complete event conflation. The bi-directional arrow between E_1 and E_2 indicates that the two events actually coalesce with each other and they are conflated in such a way that they constitutes a new lexical item (represented by E_* in Figure 5.7) as a single conceptual event.

5.6.4 *Application of Tests*

The morphosyntactic and prosodic tests proposed in this study indicate that VV compounds like resultative and directional compounds display all the typical properties of canonical SVCs. Actually they represent the prototypical case of SVCs in Mandarin Chinese.

(162) (a) *LE* **TEST**—2 not possible

*Ta   tui   **le**   dao   **le**   wo.

S/he   push   **ASP**   fall   **ASP**   me

(b) **ADVERB TEST**—2 not possible

*Ta   **jintian**   tu   **mingtian**   dao   le   wo.

S/he   **today**   push   **tomorrow**   fall   ASP   me

(c) *TA* **INSERTION**—not possible

*Ta   tui   **ta**   dao   le   wo.

S/he   push   **s/he**   fall   ASP   me

(d) **STRESS TEST**—multiple not possible

*Ta   **'tui**   **'dao**   le   wo.

S/he   **push**   **fall**   ASP   me

(e) **REVERSIBILITY TEST**—irreversible

*Ta   **dao**   **tui**   le   wo.

S/he   **fall**   **push**   ASP   I

(f) *BA* **TEST**—2 not possible

*Ta   **ba**   wo   tui   le   **ba**   wo   dao   le   wo.

S/he   BA   I   push ASP   BA   I   fall   ASP   me

(g) **PAUSE TEST**—pause not possible

*Ta   tui,   (···)   dao   le   wo.

S/he   push,   fall   ASP   me

In Mandarin Chinese, the perfective aspect of a verb is often expressed by the particle *le*, which is usually attached to the verb directly as in (163a):

(163) a. Ta   tui-**le**   wo.

S/he   push-**ASP**   me

' S/he push me. '

b. *Ta   tui-**le**   dao   wo.

S/he   push-**ASP**   fall   me

The ungrammaticality of (163b) shows that it is impossible to insert an aspectual particle between *tui* and *dao*, which indicates that these two verbs behave like a verb complex rather than two individual verbs.

Structures with VV compounds like examples in (162) only allow one *le* attachment to the final verb because VV strings in these structures act like one single conceptual unit. The entire compound only allows one temporal adverb specification and one *ba* construction, which indicates that two verbs in VV compounds do not display the properties as two separate verbs. It is impossible to insert *ta* or a pause between the two verbs and the entire compound can only receive one main stress. It also lacks reversibility. Therefore, VV compounds like resultative and directional compounds pass all of the tests for SVCs. They demonstrate high degrees of verb serialization and complete event conflation. Thus, they are justified in situating at the far end of event dependence, as illustrated in Figure 4.1.

5.7 Discussion

As it has been mentioned earlier, constructions with multiple verbs are potentially ambiguous in Mandarin Chinese. Whether a particular construction is eligible for interpretation as an SVC or not depends on whether it abides by the three iconically based semantic principles proposed in this study. Coordinated clauses like (1) mainly violate the principle of situational interdependence while clausal complements like (2) usually violate both the principle of situational interdependence and the principle of temporary sequence. The other three constructions like (3), (4), and (5) conform to all of the three semantic principles and thus they qualify as SVCs.

The five constructions display a continuum of event (in) dependence. Coordinated clauses like (1) reflect the highest degree of event independence between two VPs or events while VV compounds like (5) represent the highest degree of event conflation. Accordingly, coordinated clauses can pass none of the morphosyntactic tests for SVCs proposed in this study, while VV compounds can withstand all of these tests. On the other hand, clausal complements like (2) cannot pass the SVC tests while purposive complements like (3) and double-headed constructions like (4) generally can. Table 5.1 summarizes the behavior of the five constructions with regard to the seven tests.

Table 5.1   Application of seven tests to the five constructions

	(1) coordinated clause construction	(2) clausal complement construction	(3) purposive complement construction	(4) double-headed construction	(5) VV compound construction
le test (two possible)	Yes	Yes	No	No	No
temporal adverb test (two possible)	Yes	Yes	No otherwise the focus will be changed	Marginally acceptable	No
ta test (ta insertion possible)	Yes	Yes	No	No	No
stress test (two possible)	Yes	Yes	No	No	No
reversibility test(reversible VPs	Yes	Yes but change the focus	No	No	No
ba test (two possible)	Yes	N/A	Yes but change the meaning	No	No
pause test (pause possible)	Yes	?	No	No	No

It has been noticed that there is a delicate interaction between lexical items and the construction types they enter into. In coordinated clauses, V_1 and V_2 are completely open lexically and virtually any kind of verb can be inserted. Usually we cannot discern any interdependence between the two VPs or the events they designate. In clausal complements, V_1 is lexically restricted, being mainly cognitive or communicative verbs, while V_2 is relatively open. In purposive complements, V_1 and V_2 are relatively open; however, they must bear some purposive relationship. In double-headed constructions, both V_1 and V_2 are mainly action and transitive verbs. In this type of construction, both verbs act on or affect the same participant. A tighter purposive relationship has been established between two verbs in this construction. In VV(V) compounds, the V_1 is relatively open while V_2 V_3 are quite restricted lexically. In SVCs with resultative complements, V_2 are mainly phase verbs or achievement verbs while in SVCs with directional complements V_2 are basically transportation verbs or transaction (dislocation) verbs. The V_3 in VVV compounds are highly restricted lexically. They are motion verbs and only about eight verbs fall into this category in Mandarin.

The semantic principles and morphosyntactic tests allow us to determine the eligibility of the five constructions in question to be considered as SVCs or non-SVCs. The analysis based on the three principles can be extended to other types of constructions and thus its descriptive power can be increased. An analysis of causative constructions (pivotal constructions) is a good case in point.

A causative construction has the canonical form $[NP_1 \ V_1 \ NP_2 \ VP_2]$ with the NP_2 serving logically both as the object of V_1 and subject of V_2. In causative constructions typically the first event occurs before the second event; for instance in the sentence: *Wo qing ni lai* 'I ask you to come', my asking occurs first and your coming takes place afterward if the event (your coming) is to apply. Therefore, such constructions abide by the principle of temporal sequence.

(164) *Wo   bi   ta   tiaowu.*

　　　I   force   3SGF   dance

　　　'I force her to dance.'

(165) *Wo   qing   ni   bangmang.*

　　　Wo   ask   you   help

　　　'I ask you to help.'

In sentence (164), *ta* 'she' logically is both the object of *bi* 'force' and subject of *tiaowu* 'dance' while in sentence (165), *ni* 'you' logically is both the object of *qing* 'ask' and the subject of *banbmang* 'help'. This construction behaves quite differently from pure clausal complements such as *Wo shuo ni jiu zou* 'I say that you go right away'. With cognitive and communicative verbs such as *shuo* 'say', *xiang* 'think' it is possible to add as an afterthought form such as *Ni jiu zuo*, *wo shuo* 'You should go right away, I say'. However, it is impossible to form sentences in this way with pivotal (causative) constructions: * *Ni jiu zuo*, *wo qing* 'You go right away, I ask' (Chao, 1968). The fact that the pivot itself is also the object of the first verb can be seen when it is repeated as a resumptive pronoun and put back in the afterthought form. The resulting sentence would be grammatical again, for instance: *Ni jiu zuo*, *wo qing **ni*** '**You** should go, I ask **you**'.

In pivotal (causative) constructions the event denoted by the second verb phrase can be regarded as a process and it is dependent on the first verb in the sense that it is causally related to the first verb. In example (165), what I'm asking is for you to help me. So your helping is more like a potential event and may not have yet been realized when the speaker makes the request. In the case that a speaker asks for help the hearer can offer help or turn the request down. When the event denoted by the second verb phrase becomes an independent one, the conceptual distance between the first verb and the second verb will be increased and usually some extra grammatical elements such as a conjunction will be called for to join these two clauses.

(166) *Wo qing ta bangmang (keshi) ta bu bangmang.*

     I   ask   he help   (but)   he not help

    'I asked him to help but he did not help me.'

In sentence (166) the two events can be considered as two separate ones. The dependence of the two verbs no longer exists and a connector is usually required between these two events. Such constructions can no longer be considered to be SVCs since they are iconically compatible with independent interpretation. "The linguistic separateness of an expression corresponds to the conceptual independence of the object or event which it represents" (Haiman, 1983:783).

Chao (1968) observes that, in general, pre-pivotal verbs, which precede NP$_2$ in a pivotal (causative) construction, are of the 'cause to' type whereas verbs with clauses as their objects are of the 'think, say' type. In general, there are two major types of causatives: verbal causatives as in (165) and unspecific causatives as in (164). In verbal causatives, verbal manners of pre-pivotal verbs are specified such as *qing* 'ask', *quan* 'persuade', *gudong* 'incite', *jianyi* 'advise' and *yaoqing* 'invite' while in unspecific causatives, the manners of pre-pivotal verbs are generally unspecified such as *bi* 'force', *shi* 'cause', *rang* 'let, cause', *qiangzhi* 'compel' and *qushi* 'drive'. Verbal causatives differ from unspecific causatives in that the event denoted by the downstairs verb is defeasible while the event denoted by the downstairs verb in unspecific causatives is usually indefeasible. In (165), I asked him to help but it is feasible that he would not help while in (164), I forced her to dance and it is not very feasible that she would not dance.

The causative constructions are construed according to the principle of temporary sequence. The two VPs have the inter-verbal NP as their shared participant and there exists a purposive relationship between them. As a result, they qualify as SVCs. However, the purposive relationship in unspecific causatives is tighter than that in verbal causatives. Accordingly, the degree of verb serialization is higher in unspecific causatives than in verbal causatives.

Chapter Six

Coverb Constructions

In this study, I will also explore coverb constructions (hence CoVCs) and the differences between SVCs and CoVCs. In Modern Mandarin, coverbs are terms created to cover a set of words which are semantically like prepositions in English (Li & Thompson 1974) and this deverbalized category has undergone or is undergoing the process of grammaticalization. Coverbs are said to be historically derived from verbs and some of them are derived from serial verb constructions. Many of the items can be used either as lexical verbs or coverbs (i. e. , many of them are homophonous with lexical verbs).

Table 6.1 lists some representative items with glosses of both their verbal meanings and their prepositional meanings.

Table 6.1   Some representative coverbs

Coverb	(Older) Verbal Meaning	Prepositional Meaning
bei	to cover, to receive	by - passive marker
ba	to take, grasp	preverbal object marker
gei	to give	benefactive 'for', dative 'to' etc.
gen	to follow	comitative 'with'
bi	to compare	than
wei	to do	benefactive 'for'
dao	to arrive	to (location)
dui	to face	to, toward

续表

Coverb	(Older) Verbal Meaning	Prepositional Meaning
xiang	to face	to, toward
shun	to follow, obey	along
yan	to go along	along
ti	to replace	on behalf on
na	to use	with

6.1 *Traditional Criteria*

Traditional analyses that coverbs are not true verbs but prepositions are based on both syntactic and semantic criteria (Poteet 1988). The following are three main syntactic criteria to distinguish coverbs from true verbs:

i) Verbs occur in the V-not-V structure while coverbs usually do not. In Mandarin Chinese, the V(erb)-not-V(erb) structure is one way to form a yes-no question.

ii) Verbs can take 'aspect' particles such as *le* 'perfective', *zhe* 'progressive' while coverbs do not.

iii) Transitive verbs may occur without overt object NPs immediately following them in answer to a yes-no question while coverbs may not.

The semantic criteria are that sentences with two true verbs denote two distinct actions while sentences with coverbs only express one action (Li & Thompson 1981).

6.2 *Problematic Criteria*

Criteria to distinguish coverbs from true verbs are problematic because there are quite a few exceptions for these criteria. First, let us look at the problematic syntactic criteria.

i) Almost all coverbs may occur in V-not-V constructions to form questions, though some sound more natural than others.

(167) a. *Ni   na   bu   na   kaizi   chi   fan?*
　　　　　You   take   not   take   chopstick eat   meal
　　　　　'Do you take (use) chopsticks to eat the meal?

　　　b. *Ni   gei   bu   gei   ta   mai   pingguo?*
　　　　　You   give   not   give   3SGM buy   apple
　　　　　'Do you buy apple for him?'

　　　c. *Ni   gen   bu   gen   ta   qu   Beijing?*
　　　　　You   follow not   follow him   go   Beijing
　　　　　'Do you go to Beijing with him?'

　　　d. *Ni   ba   bu   ba   shu   gei   wo?*
　　　　　you   OBJ not   OBJ book   give   me
　　　　　'Do you give me the book?' (sometimes pose a threat)

　　　e. *? Ta   bei   bu   bei   mifeng   yao   le?*
　　　　　He   BEI   not   BEI   bee   bite   PERF
　　　　　? 'Was he stung by bees?' (indicate willingness to be bit such as for medical treatments)

　　　As (167) illustrates, the typical coverbs like instrumental *na*, benefactive *gei*, comitative *gen*, object marker *ba*, passive *bei* can enter into V-not-V constructions to form questions.

ii) It has also been noticed that a number of coverbs can allow (e. g. *dui* 'toward', *xiang* 'to') or even requires (e. g. *shun* 'along', *yan* 'along') the particle *zhe*. *Wei* 'for' allows both *zhe* and *le*. (Li & Thompson 1974; Poteet 1988)

(168) a. *Ta   dui   zhe   diren   kai   qiang.*
　　　　　He   toward PROG   enemy   fire gun
　　　　　'He fired his gun (toward) at enemies. '

　　　b. *Ta   yan   zhe   he   an   zuo.*

He　along　　PROG　river　bank　　walk

'He is going along a river bank. '

c. ***Wei le/zhe***　　*renmim de liyi*,　*ta xianchu le*　*shengming*.

For PERF/PROG people　of　interest　he give up PERF life

'He sacrificed his life for people's cause. '

The traditional semantic criteria to distinguish coverbs from lexical verbs are also problematic. Problems with the semantic criteria are the lack of precision in explaining the term 'action' (Poteet 1988).

i) First, stative and adjectival verbs in Mandarin do not express actions but they are included in the verb category.

(169) *Wo*　*pengyou*　*hen*　　*congming*.

My　friend　very　　clever

'My friend (is) very clever. '

In (169), the adjectival verb *congming* does not signal any action; however, it functions as a verb to be a predicate in this sentence.

ii) Second, it is not clear if verbs like *kaishi* (begin), *tingzhi* (stop) should be considered as denoting separate actions from their complements (Poteet 1988).

(170) *Ta*　*tingzhi*　*le*　　　*chouyan*.

He　stop　　PERF　smoke

'He has stopped smoking. '

No one has ever proposed that ' *tingzhi* ' should be considered as a coverb, but in what sense is the stopping of an action a separate action from the action that one is stopping?

iii) Thirdly, serial verb constructions (SVCs) do not usually denote two distinct actions. Often the information status of the constituents of SVCs is reduced, and the separate verbs do not denote individuated actions (Frawley 1992).

(171) *Ta*　*yong*　　*kuaizi*　　*chi*　*fan*.

He　use　　chopstick　eat　　meal

'He uses chopsticks to eat his meal. '

　　According to traditional analyses, *yong* is usually regarded as a verb and thus the construction in (171) is viewed as an SVC. However, the two verb phrases: *yong kaizi* 'use chopsticks' and *chi fan* 'eat meals' do not constitute two individuated actions.

　　Yin (2001) claims that SVCs reflect degrees of event conflation. SVCs are generally construable as two causally connected phases of a single event as the following example indicates.

(172) *Ta* **tui** **dao** *le* *yi* *zhang* *zuozi*.

　　　He push fall PERF a CL table.

　　'He has pushed down a table.'

　　In (172), the two serial verbs *tui* 'push' and *dao* 'fall' do not denote two distinct actions, but signal a single event with two connected phases.

6.3 *Verbhood Tests*

　　It has been noticed that there are coverbs which display characteristics of verbs. Also it can be found that certain verbs can not stand some of the verbhood tests.

　　For instance, there are verbs which do not allow some or all of the aspect particles (e. g. *xiang* 'resemble' as in (173) does not take *le*, *zhe*; *si* 'die' does not allow *zhe*; *gei* 'give' as in (174), *song* 'send' and *ji* 'post' usually do not take *zhe*) (Poteet 1988).

(173) a. *Ta* **xiang** *ta* *baba*.

　　　　He resemble his dad.

　　　　'He resembles his dad.'

　　 b. ** Ta* **xiang** *le/zhe* *ta* *baba*.

　　　　He resemble PERF/PROG his dad.

(174) a. *Ta* **gei** **le** *wo* *yi* *ben* *shu*.

　　　　He give PERF me one CL book

　　　　'He has given me a book.'

b. *Ta **gei** **zhe** wo yi ben shu.

He give PROG me one CL book

The evidence that some verbs do not pass some of the verbhood tests suggests that these verbs may have characteristics shared by some of the coverbs.

6.4 Present Analysis

6.4.1 Coverbs—A Continuum

To accommodate these coverb phenomena, I will use a cognitive approach to argue that structurally similar and underspecified constructions in Mandarin display a continuum of interpretation and syntactic behavior. The class of coverbs is neither a discrete nor homogenous class. In modern Mandarin, coverbs generally cannot be used alone as lexical verbs since they serve mainly to predicate relations between two nouns or between a verb and an oblique object as do prepositions in English. However, most coverbs still have some properties of verbs. Thus, coverbs lie on a continuum between verbs and prepositions. Coverbs could be viewed as relational predications occupying different points in different constructions along a continuum between verbs and prepositions. Their position is partly determined by morphosyntactic tests for verb-hood.

Na (' take ' — instrumental), *gen* (' follow ' — comitative) can pass more tests of this kind: aspectual tests such as *le*, *zhe*, and the V-not-V test, which suggests that coverbs of this kind are relatively closer to the verbal end while *ba* (object marker) and *bei* (passive) pass fewer verbhood tests, which indicates that these coverbs are relatively closer to the prepositional end (Yin 2003).

(175) a. Ta na **le/zhe** kaizi chi fan.

He take PERF/PROG chopstick eat meal

'He ate/is eating his meal with chopsticks. '

b. *Ta   na   bu   na   kaizi   chi fan?*

He   take   not   take   chopstick   eat meal

'Does he eat his meal with chopsticks?'

(176)a. *Ta* ***ba*** ***le/zhe***   *fan*   *chi diao*   *le.*

He   OBJ   PERF/PROG   meal   eat finish   PERF

b. *? Ta* ***ba*** ***bu*** ***ba*** *fan* *chi diao*   *le?*

He   OBJ not OBJ meal   eat finish   PERF

(177) a. *Fan* ***bei*** ***le/zhe***   *ta chi*   *diao*   *le.*

meal   BEI PERF/PROG   he eat   finish   PERF

b. *? Fan* ***bei*** ***bu*** ***bei*** *ta* *chi diao* *le?*

meal   BEI not BEI he   eat finish PERF

'Was the meal eaten by him?'

However, the positions for coverbs to be in the continuum are not fixed and they are quite flexible. They could enter into various constructions to express different meanings.

(178) *Ta* ***na*** *zhe* *tiaogen* *chi fan.*

He   take   PROG   spoon   eat meal

'He is taking the spoon to eat his meal. '

With the aspectual marker *zhe*, the verb flavor is enhanced and *na* in this construction will be pulled much closer to the verbal end.

In fact, grammatical elements are meaningful. The problems with previous analyses mainly come from questionable assumptions about meaning and grammatical categories, which claim that grammatical particles are semantically empty morphemes used exclusively to indicate different syntactic structures and that the ability of a word to enter into a given construction is independent of its meaning (Poteet 1988).

Langacker (1987, 1991) maintains that linguistic categorizations and conceptual categorizations are not independent and constructions and grammatical markers are meaningful. With the help of grammatical markers it could induce different interpretations and thus the language user could make a particular coverb more like a verb or more like a preposition through different means such as with or without an aspectual marker.

6.4.2 Entities Undergoing Process

Coverbs are said to be developed from true verbs. Changes from verbs to coverbs to indicate grammatical functions do not stop at present and some members of this class are still in the onging process of grammaticalization. So coverbs should be viewed as entities undergoing process rather than as static objects.

For example, some so-called case markers like *ba* 'object marker', *bei* 'agent (passive) marker', *na* 'instrumental marker', *gei* 'dative marker' are still going on grammaticalization.

(179) *Wo*　**ba**　*hua*　*ping*　**dapo**　*le.*

　　　I　　OBJ　flower　bottle　break　PERF

　　　'I have **broken** the flower bottle (vase)'

Ba constructions indicate total affectedness of patients and they are originally used with verbs of high transitivity like *dapo* 'break'. Now it is possible for a non-high transitive verb to enter into *ba* constructions in modern Mandarin as the following example illustrates.

(180) *Wo*　**ba**　*shu*　**du**　*le*　*liang*　*bian.*

　　　I　　OBJ　book　read　PERF　two　times

　　　'I have read the book twice.'

6.5 Metaphorical and Functional Extensions

The distribution of a word or a morpheme is associated with its meaning and a particular word or construction may have a range of interrelated meanings. In contrary to traditional analyses to analyze different senses of a linguistic item independently I would like to discuss the interrelatedness of its verb use and its coverb use and explore motivations behind its metaphorical and functional extensions.

6.5.1 Na 'take' — Instrumental and Topic Marker

In using something, usually we should take it and then manipulate it or perform actions with it. So *na* focuses on an initial portion of the action chain of 'take-and-then-do'. It is a good candidate to serve as an instrumental marker since the case of using something often involves the situation to take the instrument first. The semantic value of using the instrument is compatible with the meaning of *na* which focuses on an initial portion in an action chain: 'take-do' (take-and-then-do).

In modern Chinese, *na* can still be used as a full lexical verb:

(181) Wo   cong   bingxiang li   **na**   pingguo.

　　　 I   from   fridge   inside   take   apple

　　　 'I took apples from the fridge. '

(182) **Na**   zhe ge fangfa jiejue   wenti.

　　　 Take (with)this CL   method solve   problem.

　　　 'Solve the problem with this method. '

These two examples illustrate two extreme cases of the uses of *na* along a continuum, with typical serial verb use as in (181) at one end and prototypical instrumental marker use as in (182) at the other end.

In addition to be used as a real transfer verb or as an instrumental marker, *na* can act as a topic marker. Taking something implies the concept of contact with it. When the transfer verb is used metaphorically to indicate mental contact, the energy transferred is in the abstract domain, i. e. , from human mind to the thing to be contacted. The topic marker comes into being when *na* 'take' indicates mental contact as in (183) and the thing to be taken and picked up serves as a reference point.

(183) **Na**   shuiguo   er yian,   wo   zui xihuan pingguo.

　　　 topic   markerfruit par talk   I   most like   apple

　　　 'Talking about fruits, I like apples best. '

6.5.2 *Ba* — *Object Marker*

Ba — the transfer verb *ba* in Old Chinese maybe is better to be interpreted as 'take hold of'. It implies certain duration of an action and the profiled portion is on the later stage — 'the holding part'. The meaning of this verb includes the concept of manipulation of objects and the end stage of an action chain and thus, it indicates completion of affectedness (Sun 1996). In the use of *ba* as object marker, the semantics of *ba* is bleached but traces of the meaning of *ba* as a transfer verb are carried over. In fact, the use of *ba* as an object marker can be viewed as a semantic/functional extension of this transfer verb.

In Mandarin *ba* is now basically used as a coverb; however, the speaker can use some means such as aspectual markers to turn it into a main verb again as the following example shows.

(184) *Ta* ***ba***   *zhe*   *men*   *bu*   *rang wo jin.*

      He   takehold of PROG   door   not   let   me enter

      ' He was taking hold of the door not to let me in. '

6.5.3 *Gei* (*give*) — *Recipient Marker and Benefactive Use*

Different meanings of *gei* ' give ' though unpredictable, are indeed motivated and related. The typical case of *gei* ' give ' is that somebody who has something passes it with his hands to anther person.

In addition to be used as a full verb, *gei* can function as a recipient marker. The recipient marker *gei* invokes a scene in which some transfer takes place. It is used to plot the path of an object sent by an agent to a recipient though it has the same base as its lexical verb use which includes a giver, a thing, and a recipient (Newman 1993, 1996).

(185) *Wo* ***gei***   *ta*   *ji*   *le*   *yi feng*   *xin.*

      I   give (to) him   send   PERF one CL   letter

      ' I sent a letter to him. '

Another grammatical function of *gei* is its benefactive use, meaning for the sake of somebody, or to the benefit of somebody. There are some connections between the recipient use and the benefactive use. The benefactive sense is to the recipient advantage. The situation whereby giving something results in some kind of benefit to the recipient is a natural and frequent occurrence in human experience (Newman 1993). When *gei* is used as a benefactive marker it usually occurs before the main verb.

(186) *Wo* *gei*   *ta*   *shengqing* *le*   *tushu* *ka.*

    I   give (for) him   apply for   PERF library card.

    'I applied for a library card for him.'

As illustrated, some linguistic items like *na*, *ba*, *gei* can be used either as lexical verbs or coverbs. Their lexical use and coverb use and various senses within coverbs are interrelated. All the senses of a particular item are far from random and that all the variants, non-central, peripheral meanings and semantic/functional extensions are related to its basic meaning (Lakoff 1987).

6.6 *Differences Between SVCs and CoVCs*

Most coverb constructions have quite different characteristics from those of prototypical SVCs but boundaries between these two constructions are not clear cut.

Serial verb constructions and coverb constructions are mainly different in event structures, more specifically in its profiling. Langacker (1988) proposes that a semantic structure derives its value through the imposition of a profile on a base. As the basis for its meaning, an expression evokes a certain body of conceptual content, called its base. Within its overall conception, it directs attention to some particular substructure — the profile. The profile comprises those portions of the base which the entity designates or refers to. "Some facet of the base is invariably raised to a distinctive level of prominence, and serves as its focal point; this substructure is the predication's profile" (Langacker, 1988: 59).

| Base | husband | wife | couple |

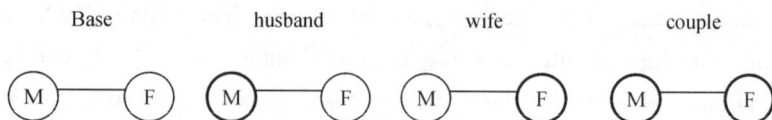

Figure 6. 1

The meanings for *husband*, *wife* and *couple* have the same base: a male (M) and a female (F) who have a certain kind of relationship indicated by a line connecting them. Although these three expressions share the same base (content), they differ in meaning by imposing different profiles indicated by boldface in Figure 6.1.

Similar to *couple*, in which both M and F are profiled, SVCs have two events which are both profiled and they are connected by some purposive or causative relationship. In coverb constructions, the event denoted by the main verb is profiled while the event denoted by the coverb is not profiled and is non-salient.

However, to a large extent, the bases for SVCs and coverb constructions are the same. The verb which is not profiled in coverb constructions thus becomes a coverb as the following two examples indicate.

(187) Wo   wei   ta   **mai** le   yi ben   shu. (*purposive*)
     I   do (for) him   buy PERF one CL   book.
     'I bought a book for him. '

(188) Ta **yan**   zhe   he   an   **zuo**.
     He follow (along) PROG river bank   walk
     'He walked along a river bank. ' (path for the profiled verb *zuo* 'walk')

In (187), *wei* is not profiled as a verb and it indicates the purpose for the profiled verb *mai* while in (188) the coverb *yan* is also not profiled as a verb and it serves as path for the profiled motion verb *zuo*.

Though the boundaries between SVCs and CoVCs are not clear cut, most CoVCs have quite different characteristics from those of canonical SVCs. SVCs and CoVCs differ mainly in their event structure, more specifically, in their profiling. SVCs have two (sub) events which are both profiled and they are connected by some purposive or causative relationship. In coverb constructions, the event denoted by the main verb is profiled while the event denoted by the coverb is largely not profiled and is non-salient. This is because the meaning of the coverb in CoVCs is not fully compositional in the sense that the whole does not equal to the sum of its parts. Maybe due to their high frequency, coverbs (as compared to SVCs) have become more schematic in meaning or they profile the participants rather than the action. So in many cases, the profile of the composite structure does not include anything but a highly schematic portion of the profile of the coverb. In fact, the continuum of verbness reflected in coverb constructions could be a continuum of the degree to which the profile of the coverb is " preserved ". Since in composite structures coverbs are largely not profiled, coverb phrases tend to serve as modifiers for main verbs or indicate grammatical functions like case marking in Modern Mandarin.

Chapter Seven

Psycholinguistic Experiments

In order to provide supporting evidence for the degree of event (in) dependence (suggested by these morphosyntactic tests) affecting different interpretations of multi-verb constructions in Mandarin Chinese and for the non-categorical nature of linguistic units, a psycholinguistic study was developed whereby native speakers of Mandarin conducted two experiments and rated complex sentences, including the five sentence types which have been just discussed. The scale of ratings is as follows:

Table 7.1   The scale of ratings of event conflation

	2 events	Between 2 events and 1 event										1 event
Scale	2	1.9	1.8	1.7	1.6	1.5	1.4	1.3	1.2	1.1	1	
Your Rating												

7.1 *Experiment One*

There were 42 native Mandarin speakers who participated in this experiment. There were 5 tokens for each of these 5 sentence types and 15 distractors. Participants were asked to assign the score 2 to a sentence which refers to two events conceptually and assign 1 to a sentence which refers to one event conceptually. They could choose scores between 1 and 2 because sentences will probably fall in the range between 1 and 2 events.

Table 7.2   The mean scores of event conflation of the constructions

Construction Type	Mean of the Rating
Coordinated Construction	1.82
Complement Construction	1.38
Purposive Construction	1.31
Double-headed Construction	1.26
VV compound Construction	1.14

The mean scores of these five sentence types conform to our predictions of the continuum of event (in) dependence. Coordinated clauses were rated as the lowest degree of event conflation while VV compounds were rated as the highest degree of event conflation.

Table 7.3   T-test value of the constructions

Two-tailed T-test	P Value
Coordinated vs. clausal complement construction	< 0.01
clausal complement vs. purposive construction	0.06
purposive vs. double-headed construction	0.058
clausal complement vs. double-headed construction	< 0.01
double headed vs. VV compound construction	< 0.01

Two-tailed t-tests show that the differences between coordinated constructions vs. clausal complement constructions, clausal complement constructions vs. double-headed constructions and double-headed constructions vs. VV compounds are all highly significant. The differences between clausal complement constructions vs. purposive constructions and purposive constructions vs. double-headed constructions are marginally significant.

The experimental results indicate that Mandarin speakers are sensitive to sentences exhibiting different degrees of event conflation. The mean scores suggest that coordinated clauses (mean: 1. 82) are situated at the far end of event independence while VV compounds (mean: 1. 14) are at the far end of event conflation.

7.2 *Experiment Two*

This experiment is designed to test the effect of the number of mention of subjects in clausal complement constructions and the number of mention of objects in double-headed constructions. The example sentences are the following:

(189) a. ***Ta***   *chengren*   *zuo*   *cuo*   *le.*
        S/he   confess   do   wrong   ASP

   b. ***Ta***   *chengren* ***ta***   *zuo cuo*   *le.*
        S/he   confess   s/he   do   wrong   ASP

(190) a. *Ta* *zhong* ***cai***   *mai.*
        S/he plant   vegetable sell

   b. *Ta*   *zhong* ***cai***   *mai* ***cai***.
        S/he   plant   vegetable sell   vegetable

The participants were divided into two groups and each of which were 30 native Mandarin speakers. There were 12 items for each sentence type. In order to avoid using the same items in the sub-types with the same subject, group A will go through item 1 to 6 with one mention of subjects or objects and go through item 7 to item 12 with two mentions of them. Group B will go through items 7 to 12 with one mention of subjects or objects and items 1 to 6 with 2 mentions of them. There were 24 testing sentences and 16 distractors.

Table 7. 4   The mean scores of event conflation of the constructions

	1 ta (subj)	2 ta's (subj)	1 obj	2 obj's
Group A	1. 409	1. 421	1. 252	1. 508
Group B	1. 372	1. 415	1. 324	1. 568
A + B	1. 391	1. 418	1. 288	1. 538

Table 7. 5   T-test value of the constructions

Two-tailed T-test	P Value
1 ta vs. 2 ta's in the constructions	0. 246
1 obj vs. 2 obj's in the constructions	< 0. 01

As mentioned previously, the 5 constructions are a matter of construal. According to communicative needs, speakers can manipulate the kind of interpretation by different means such as the absence or presence of the resumptive third person (s) *ta (men)* or the object in downstairs clauses. The t-test statistic indicates that there is no significant difference between 1 *ta* and 2 *ta*'s versions of clausal complement constructions because it does not cause ambiguity or invite a different interpretation whether the second *ta* is absent or present. However, when the object in double-headed constructions is restored it is possible to cause ambiguity and invite a different interpretation from a purposive to a coordinated interpretation. Consequently, the difference between 1 mention of an object and 2 mentions of objects is significant.

In this study, the experiments were designed to explore the phenomenon of event autonomy or event conflation of the five [V (N) V ...] types and the effects of construal on the interpretation of different constructions. The findings in the experiments suggest that Mandarin speakers are sensitive to sentences exhibiting different degrees of event conflation. The results in the experiments indicate that event conflation really turned out to be a graded rather than a discrete phenomenon.

Chapter Eight

The Association of Multi-Verb Constructions with Verbs

To date, most of the published analyses of Mandarin Chinese SVCs have relied on constructed examples or on the intuition of speakers/ linguists. Unfortunately, there has been little or no systematic exploration of actual data of Mandarin multi-verb sequences from Mandarin Chinese corpora. One of the major objectives of this study is to fill in this gap. Instead of recycling old examples from previous analyses, this study mined actual examples from the Lancaster Corpus of Mandarin Chinese to explore multi-verb constructions (MVCs) which contain two or more verbs in a sequence and the interaction between lexical items and the construction types. The Lancaster Corpus of Mandarin Chinese (LCMC), a publicly available balanced corpus, was designed as a Chinese match for the FLOB and FROWN corpora of modern British and American English. The LCMC sampled 15 written text genres including news, literary texts, academic prose, and official documents, published in the People's Republic of China in the 1990s. Following FLOB/ FROWN, the corpus contains five hundred 2,000-word samples taken disproportionally from 15 genres in written Mandarin Chinese, totaling one million words.

The corpus data for this study were obtained exclusively from the LCMC. I obtained the 50 most frequent verbs, the tokens of which occur no fewer than 300 times, and searched them as key words using the web-based concordancer. If the number of the hits which were obtained using a particular key verb search was greater than 300, I randomized the results to get 300 hits. The 15,000 hits which I obtained in this way (50 key verbs multiplied by 300 tokens) form the basis of my corpus analysis. Each clause which contains the key word (verb) in the query hit was individually examined in the context of its sentence to see if it was a multi-verb sequence. The range of multi-verb sequences which were identified from the corpus searches is broad and covers a wide range of construction types. However, this chapter will focus on the five construction types under discussion. The corpus results indicate that there is a delicate interaction between lexical items and the construction types they enter into. The results also show that there are degrees of attraction of verbs to different multi-verb constructions. In this chapter, I will explore the association of verbs with particular constructions, that is, what verbs enter into a given construction type, as evidenced from the corpus data. I will go through each major construction type which was discussed in Chapter Five.

8.1 *Coordinate Construction*

There are 45 instances of coordinate constructions with shared subjects with the corpus returns. Among them, there are 21 cases in which no connector or punctuation exists between two verbs and 24 cases in which there is a unique punctuation " 、 " which is called *dun hao* in Chinese. The pause duration for this punctuation is shorter than that of English comma. Unlike the English commas, Chinese commas can conjoin two clauses. In Chinese, if two verbs appear before and after a comma, they are more likely to be interpreted as two clauses and to form a clause chain, and thus, they are not interpreted as potential SVCs or MVCs. However, a *dun hao* is not generally considered to link two clauses, but instead is viewed as linking two coordinated phrases. Thus, I would like to include a sequence of verbs containing this intervening punctuation as one of many special types of MVCs explored in this study.

Among the 24 instances of coordination with the intervening punctuation *dun hao*, there are 20 different verbs occupying the V1 position. Both transitive verbs and intransitive verbs can fill the V1 position. Both concrete verbs such as *da* 'strike' and abstract verbs such as *anwei* 'comfort' can serve as the V1 in this kind of coordination. Actually there are two verbs, whose frequency is more than one as Figure 8. 1 illustrates. The two verbs are *chi* 'eat' and *yanjiu* 'study, research', whose frequency is three for each. The relatively high frequency of *chi* 'eat' here might be due to the fact that *eating* is a very common verb since it reflects a basic and essential need for human beings. As for the V2 position, no two verbs are identical in this slot in this kind of construction, that is, all 24 verbs in the V2 position among the 24 instances are different.

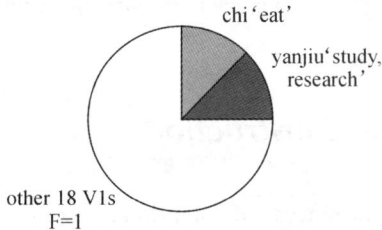

chi 'eat'

yanjiu 'study, research'

other 18 V1s
F=1

Figure 8. 1   Frequency of V1s in coordinate constructions with a '*dun hao*'

In the 21 cases of coordination without any intervening connector or punctuation, there are 15 different V1 verbs, three of which have a frequency more than one, as Figure 8. 1 shows.

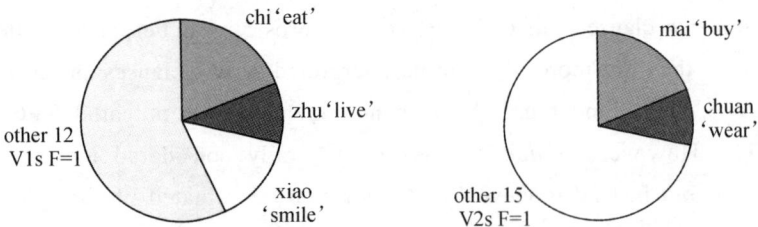

chi 'eat'

zhu 'live'

other 12
V1s F=1

xiao 'smile'

mai 'buy'

chuan 'wear'

other 15
V2s F=1

Figure 8. 2   Frequency of V1s and V2s in coordinate constructions without a '*dun hao*'

There are 2 instances for *zhu* 'live (in a house) ' , 4 cases of *chi* 'eat' and 3 cases of *xiao* 'smile, laugh'. The 9 instances from the LCMC which contain these verbs as V1 are in (191).

(191) a. *tamen   que neng   xi   **xiao**   nu   ma*

they   but can   happily   **laugh**   angrily   curse

'but they can laugh happily and curse angrily'

b. *jiguan de   zhanshimen gaoxingdi **xiao**   zhe   tiao   zhe*

office GEN soldiers   happily   **laugh** PROG jump PROG

'the soldiers in the office were happily laughing and jumping'

c. *shouli   mei   qian   **xiao**   bu   dong   xi   bu   cheng*

in hand NEG money **laugh** NEG move   be happy NEG achieve

'with no money in hand (people) are not able to laugh and be happy'

d. *xianzai   dajia   dou   zai   guangchang shang   **chi***

Now   everyone   all   at   public squareup   **eat**

ya   shui   de

INJ   sleep   PRT

'Now everyone eat and sleep on the public square'

e. *Anying 、 Anqing   yu   dongshi   yijia   laoshao*

Anying, *Anqing* with Mr. Dong   one family   old young

*tong   **chi**   tong   zhu*

together **eat**   together live

'Anying, Anqing ate together and lived together with Mr. Dong's family of the old and the young'.

f. *women niangermen   **chi** bu   shang chuang bu   shang*

we   mother and children **eat** NEG up   wear   NEG up

'we mother and children have no food to eat and no clothes to wear'

g. *rang   haizimen   **chi**   bao   chuan   nuan*

let   children   **eat**   full   wear   warm

'let the children have enough to eat and wear warmly'

h. *jiajia*   ***zhu***   *xin fang   mai   dianshi*
   every family   **live**   new house buy   TV
   ' every family lived in new houses and bought TVs '

i. *ta   he ta ...   **zhu**   yang   fang   zuo   xiao   qiche*
   3SGF and 3SGM   **live**   foreign   house ride   small   car
   ' she and he live in the villa and ride in cars '

It is understandable that *zhu* ' live (in a house) and *chi* ' eat ' are common verbs since they represent two everyday human activities. The relatively high frequency of *xiao* ' smile, laugh ' is also due to the fact that it is a common human behaviour. Amongst the 21 cases of comma-less coordination, there are 17 different verbs in the V2 position. There are four cases of the verb *mai* ' buy ' and it seems that this verb easily enters into the V2 position in this kind of coordination. All in all, the verbs that fill either the V1 or V2 position in these two kinds of coordination are quite varied. The frequency for the majority of the verbs is only 1. As discussed previously, coordinate constructions reflect the limiting case of event independence.

8.2 *Complement Construction*

Complement constructions are very common among multi-verb constructions. There are 654 instances of complement constructions from the search results. Some examples of complement constructions from the LCMC are in (192).

(192) a. *Zuoquan   **kaishi**   **zou**   xiang   shehui*
       Zuoquan   **begin**   **walk** towards   society
       ' Zuoquan began to walk towards the society '

   b. *dangshi   ta   ji   **xiang   chengwei** " shiren "*
      at that time   3SGM mvery much **want**   **become**   " poet "
      ' at that time he wanted to become a " poet " very much '

In complement constructions, the first sub-event (denoted by V1) serves as the main event and the second sub-event (denoted by V2) serves as the complement of V1 ; that is, the second of the two sub-events bears a subordinate relationship. Table 8.1 shows the frequency ≥ 10 for the most common verbs occupying the V1 and V2 positions. In complement constructions, the verb occupying the V1 slot is much more restricted than V2 and, consequently, V2 is more varied. The type frequency of verbs in V1 is much lower than that of V2. Two verbs, *kaishi* ‘begin, start’ and *xiang* ‘think, want’, are especially frequent as V1 and these two verbs occupy more than one third (40.7%) of all the verb tokens used in the V1 position.

Table 8.1   Frequency (≥ 10) of V1 and V2 in complement constructions

Freq	V1	Freq	V2	Freq
Over 100	**kaishi** *‘begin, start’*	**143**		
	xiang *‘think, want’*	**123**		
26—50	*xuyao* ‘request, need’	49		
	yaojiu ‘require’	29		
	jinxing ‘ be going on, conduct’	28		
	tichu ‘put forward’	27		
20—25	*shi* ‘be’	24	*rang* ‘let’	21
			you ‘have, there be’	21
10—19	*shuo* ‘say’	15	*jiaqiang* ‘strengthen’	18
	zhidao ‘know’	13	*ting* ‘listen’	14
	renwei ‘ think, hold the view’	13	*chuxian* ‘ appear, come into being’	12
		11		
	jixu ‘continue’	10	*xie* ‘write’	12
	xiwang ‘hope, wish’		*fazhan* ‘develop’	12
			zuo ‘do, make’	12
			chengwei ‘become’	11
			qu ‘go’	11
			(*gou*) *mai* ‘purchase’	11
			yong ‘use’	11

续表

Freq	V1	Freq	V2	Freq
Others F < 10		169		488
Total verb tokens		654		654

In analysing what kinds of verbs are used as V1 and their relative frequency, it has been found that there are certain kinds of verbs which are used more frequently than others as Table 8. 2 indicates. In the V1 position, inchoative/inceptive verbs, continuative verbs and thinking and communicative verbs are used most frequently in complement constructions. Requesting or asking verbs also easily enter into the V1 slot of complement constructions. The seven types of verbs listed in Table 8. 2 make up 82. 1% of all the verb tokens in the V1 position. The corpus results indicate that verbs in the V1 position are quite restricted in complement constructions.

Table 8. 2　Types of V1 and their frequency for complement constructions

Types of V1	Freq
Starting or (continue to) conduct verbs	**182**
kaishi ' *begin, start* '	143
jinxing ' (*continue to*) *conduct* '	28
jixu ' *continue, go on* '	11
Thinking or communicative verbs	**161**
xiang ' think '	123
shuo ' say '	15
renwei ' think, hold '	13
other communicative verbs	10

续表

Types of V1	Freq
Requesting or asking verbs	**85**
xuyao ' require'	49
yaoqiu ' request, demand'	29
zhuiwen ' ask further'	7
Being or changing verbs	**32**
shi ' be'	24
bian ' change'	8
Psychological verbs	**30**
xiwang ' hope, wish'	10
xihuan ' like'	8
ai ' love, like'	5
pa ' fear'	3
kewang ' long for'	1
jidong ' be excited'	1
taoyan ' be loath'	1
danxin ' be worried'	1
Putting forward, proposing verb	
tichu ' put forward, proposing'	27
Knowing or sensing verbs	**20**
zhidao ' know'	13
ting ' listen'	3
kan ' look at'	3
jian ' see'	1
Total Frequency	**537**

Next, I would like to address the most frequently collocating verbs in the V2 position for complement constructions. Table 8. 3 displays collocating V2 verbs (frequence $\geqslant 2$) with the five most frequent verbs in the V1 position.

Table 8.3   Collocating V2 verbs (frequence ≥ 2) with the five most frequent verbs in the V1 position for complement constructions

V1	V2 (Freq ≥ 2)				V2 Total Freq	V2 Listed Freq	Listed V2 Freq / Total Freq
kaishi 'begin, start' 144	*chuxian* '**appear, come into being**'	9	*tan* 'explore'	5	143	52	(52/143) 36.4%
	bian 'change'	4	*you* 'have, there be'	4			
	fasheng 'take place'	4	*jin* 'enter'	3			
	fazhan 'develop'	2	*huisheng* 'rise back'	2			
	chengren 'admit'	2	*gongzuo* 'work'	2			
	yanjiu 'study, research'	2	*jie* 'receive'	2			
	renzhi 'realize'	2	*juede* 'think, feel'	2			
	jinxing 'conduct'	2	*zou* 'walk, leave'	2			
			zao 'build'	2			
xiang 'think, want' 123	*rang* '**let**'	13	*qing* 'ask'	7	123	58	(58/123) 47.2%
	zhao 'search'	6	*chengwei* '**become**'	5			
	kan 'look'	4	*ting* 'listen'	4			
	zuo 'sit'	3	*qu* 'go'	3			
	xie 'write'	3	*shangxue* 'go to school'	3			
	tiao 'jump'	3	*mai* 'buy'	3			
	lai 'come'	3	*zuo* 'do make'	3			
	chi 'eat'	3	*zhidao* 'know'	2			
	ku 'cry'	2	*shuo* 'say'	2			
	dai 'take'	2	*zou* 'walk, leave'	2			
	jiehun 'get married'	2					
	tan 'speak, talk'	2					
xuyao 'request, need' 49	*you* '**have, there be**'	7	*jinxing* 'conduct'		49	24	(24/49) 49.4%
			xietiao 'coordinate'	3			
	fenxi 'analyze'	2	*fayang* 'promote'	2			
	tigao 'raise'	2	*yanjiu* 'study, research'	2			
	yong 'use'	2					
	jiejue 'solve'	2					

续表

V1	V2 (Freq ≥ 2)				V2 Total Freq	V2 Listed Freq	Listed V2 Freq / Total Freq
yaoqiu 'require' 29	*jianli* 'set up'	2	*tigong* 'provide'	2	29	6	(6/29) 20.1%
	goumai 'purchase'	2					
jinxing 'conduct' 29	*caozuo* 'operate'	2			29	2	(2/28) 7.1%
Average							32%

In each of these five cases, it seems that there is no particular verb which typically collocates very heavily with any of these five verbs, which suggests that the verbs in the V2 position in complement constructions are more varied. However, in the case of *kaishi* 'start, begin', there is one verb, *chuxian* 'appear, come into being', which is used more frequently as V2 than any other verb is. *Rang* 'let, allow' is more likely to collocate with the verb *xiang* 'think, want'. The most frequent verb used with *xuyao* 'need, require' is *you* 'have, possess, there be', which suggests that what we often need or require is to have or possess something. There is no particular verb which is used frequently with *yaoqiu* 'request, demand' or *jinxing* '(continue to) conduct'.

Table 8.4 displays collocating V1 verbs (frequence ≥ 2) with the three most frequent verbs in the V2 position. *You* 'have, there be' as V2 is often used with the verb *xuyao* 'request, need'. *Rang* 'let' collocates frequently with the psychological verb *xiang* 'think, want'. The verb most frequently used with *jiaqiang* 'strengthen' is *tichu* 'put forward'. From the above two tables, it can be seen that the ratio of the frequency of the listed V1 (frequency ≥ 2) over the total frequency of V1 is much higher than that of the frequency of the listed V2 (frequency ≥ 2) over the total frequency of V2. This tendency is also evidenced from the overall situation for complement constructions as illustrated in Table 8.1, all of which indicates that in complement constructions, there is an asymmetry between the two verbs in that V1 is much more restricted while V2 is much more open. Complement constructions also display a semantic or conceptual imbalance. The V1 in complement constructions is more schematic while the V2 is more concrete. Such imbalance could facilitate event integration of MVCs. It is hard to integrate two separate events or two separate verbs that independently profile some events. But when one verb is doing more grammatical work and the other is doing more lexical work it can be easier to integrate the two sub-events denoted by the two verbs into a macro event.

Table 8.4　Collocating V1 verbs（frequence ≥ 2）with the three most frequent verbs in the V2 position for complement constructions

V1（Freq ≥ 2）	Freq	V2	V1 Total Freq	V1 Listed Freq	Listed V1 Freq/Total Freq
xuyao ' request, need'	7	*you* ' have, there be ' (22)	**22**	16	(16/22) 72.7%
kaishi ' begin, start'	4				
faxian ' discover, find'	3				
zhidao ' know'	2				
xiang ' think, want'	**13**	*rang* ' let' (21)	21	19	(19/21) 90.5%
youyi ' intend'	2				
tichu ' put forward'	2				
shi ' be'	2				
tichu ' put forward'	4	*jiaqiang* ' strengthen' (18)	18	14	(14/18) 77.8%
youliyu ' be useful for'	3				
jixu ' need badly'	3				
qiangdiao ' emphasize'	2				
dedao ' obtain'	2				
Average					**80.3%**

The corpus evidence indicates that in complement constructions, there is an asymmetry between the two verbs in that V1 is much more restricted while V2 is much more open. The two verbs *xiang* 'want' and *kaishi* 'begin, start' are most attracted to the V1 position in complement constructions

8.3 *Purposive Construction*

Purposive constructions are quite common among multi-verb sequences. There are 334 instances of purposive constructions from the search results. In purposive constructions, the first sub-event denoted by V1 often serves as the preparatory phase and the second sub-event denoted by V2 specifies the purpose of V1.

Table 8.5 shows V1s and V2s with frequencies > 4 for the 334 cases of purposive constructions from the LCMC search results. From Table 8.5, it can be seen that the most frequent verbs used in V1 slots in purposive constructions are *lai* 'come', *zhao* 'find, search' and *zuo* 'sit, take' while the most frequent verb used in the V2 slot to specify purpose is *kan* 'look, watch'. The motion verb *qu* 'go' is used commonly in both V1 and V2 slots in such constructions.

Table 8.5   V1 and V2 with frequencies > 4 in purposive constructions

Frequency	V1		V2	
20 and above	*lai* 'come'	31	*kan* 'look, watch'	27
	zhao 'find, search'	30	*qu* 'go'	20
	zuo 'sit, take'	23		
10—19	*qu* 'go'	11	*yanjiu* 'study, do research'	10
			xuexi 'study'	10
			mai 'buy'	10
5—9	*hua* 'spend'	8	*lai* 'come'	9
	tai 'raise, lift'	7	*zuo* 'do, make'	9
	dai(*tou*) 'carry, take the lead'	7	*shuo* (*ming*) 'say, explain'	8

续表

Frequency	V1		V2	
5—9	*xie* 'write'	7	*zou* 'walk, leave'	7
	jie 'fetch, take over'	6	*dao* 'arrive, reach'	5
	huitou 'turn one's head'	6	*jiao* 'call'	5
	mai 'buy'	5	*tan* 'talk'	5
	na 'take'	5	*chi* 'eat'	5
			gei 'give'	5

In purposive constructions, the most frequently used verb in the V1 position is *lai* 'come', as Table 8.6 shows. It seems that there is no preferred verb for the V2 position which is frequently used with the verb *lai* 'come' or with another common motion verb *qu* 'go'.

Table 8.6　Collocations of V2 with V1 (frequency > 6) in purposive constructions

V1	F	V2	F
lai 'come'	31	*yanjiu* 'study, do research'	4
		tigao 'raise, improve'	2
		fazhan 'develop'	2
		other verb types (frequency = 1):	23
zhao 'find, look for, search'	30	**communicative verbs:**	**10**
		tanhua 'talk'	5
		jiaotan 'talk to each other'	1
		shuohua 'speak (to someone)'	1
		qiuqing 'ask for mercy'	1
		lilun 'argue'	1
		pingli 'reason (with someone)'	1
		qu 'go'	3
		zuo 'do, make'	2
		other verb types (frequency = 1):	15

续表

V1	F	V2	F
zuo 'sit, take (vehicle)'	23	*qu* 'go'	3
		deng 'wait for'	2
		he 'drink'	2
		chi 'eat'	2
		xiang 'think'	2
		other verb types (frequency = 1):	12
qu 'go'	11	*ting* 'listen'	2
		other verb types (frequency = 1):	9
hua 'spend'	8	*mai* 'buy'	6
		qiuyi maiyao 'look for a doctor and buy medicine'	1
		qing zuo 'ask somebody to do something'	1
tai 'raise, lift'	7	*kan* 'look'	4
		qu kan 'go look'	1
		lai kan 'come look'	1
		rang kan 'let look'	1
xie 'write'	7	*cui* 'urge'	2
		gaobie 'say good-bye'	2
		other verb types (frequency = 1):	3
dai (*tou*) 'carry, take the lead'	7	*lai* 'come'	2
		other verb types (frequency = 1):	5

Table 8.6 shows that the purposes for the two verbs *zhao* 'find, search' and *zuo* 'sit, take (vehicle)' are also diversified; however, the verb *zhao* 'find, search' is used rather frequently with one particular type of verb: the

communicative type. There are 10 instances of communicative verbs used with *zhao* 'find, search' in purposive constructions. The verb *tai* 'raise' is used commonly with the verb *kan* 'look' or phrases with *kan* 'look'. In fact, all the verb instances used in V2 positions in Table 8.6 which collocate with *tai* 'raise' are either *kan* used as a individual verb or phrases which contain the verb *kan*. Interestingly, out of seven cases there are five objects of *tai* 'raise' are *tou* 'head'. In addition, there is one instance of *wan* 'wrist' and one instance of *jiao* 'foot' used as the object of *tai* 'raise'. Naturally, the common purpose of raising one's head is for looking. The aim of raising one's foot here from the corpus data is for letting someone have a look at the foot. In terms of objects used for the verb *hua* 'spend', all the eight objects involve the concept of money (seven cases of *qian* 'money' and one case of *jixu* 'savings'). The verb *hua* 'spend' is frequently used with the verb *mai* 'buy' or its compound. Out of eight instances of *hua* 'spend' as V1, there are six cases of *mai* 'buy' in the V2 position. The common purpose of spending money is to buy something or buy service. In fact, the only case which does not involve the verb *mai* 'buy' is *qing zuo* 'ask someone to do something', which indicates that the money is spent to buy someone's service (doing something). Some examples from the LCMC which contain *hua* 'spend' in the V1 position are given in (193).

(193) a. *yixie   qiye   yuanyi   **hua**   qian   mai   jiaoche*
   Some enterprises are willing **spend** money buy car
   'Some enterprises are willing to spend money to buy cars'

  b. *ni   yao   **hua**   yi   kuai   qian   mai   yuetaipiao   de*
   you need **spend** one yuan money buy platform ticket PRT
   'you need to spend one yuan to buy a platform ticket'

  c. *you   ren   ningyuan   "**hua** qian"   mai   shijian*
   There be people would rather "spend money" buy time
   'There are people who would rather "spend money" to buy time'

d. *ta* **hua** *jinpingsheng de*   *jixu*   *qiu yi*   *mai yao*

   3SGF **spend** up all life   GEN savingssee doctors buy medicines

   ' She spent up all her life's savings to see doctors and buy

   medicines '

e. *wo* **hua**   *qian*   *qing chengli de*   *tiejiang*   *gei*   *ta*

   I   spend money ask   city-in   GEN   blacksmith give, for him

   da   *le*   *yi*   *ba*   *xiao*   *liandao*

   strike   perf   one   CL   small   sickle

   ' I spent money to ask the blacksmith in the city to make a small

   sickle for him '

Table 8. 7 shows the collocations with verbs used in the V2 position
with frequencies > 7. The most frequently used verb in V2 positions is
the verb *kan* ' look, watch '. Verbs of posture or change of posture
(either head or body) frequently collocate with *kan*. Out of 27 instances
of V1 used together with *kan*, 14 cases involve verbs of posture or
change of posture (either head or body) , for it is often the case that
people turn their heads or bodies or stand or sit in a place to look at or
watch something. In the case of *qu* ' go' used as V2, verbs in the V1
position are quite varied and only one verb *zuo* ' take (vehicle) ' has a
frequency > 1. As for the activity denoted by the verb *yanjiu* ' study, do
research ' , one common way to study something is to hold a meeting. It
can be seen from Table 8. 7 that there are four verb phrases involving the
concept of ' meeting '. It can be seen as well that the verb phrases with
qian ' money' as the object commonly collocate with the V2 *mai* ' buy '.
One verb which I should mention here is *tan* ' have a talk ' although its
frequency is only 5. Used as a V2, *tan* frequently collocates with the
verb *zhao* ' find, look for (someone) ' , which indicates that the
preparatory phase for ' having a talk ' is often ' finding or looking for
someone '. In fact, in the 5 instances of *tan* as V2 in purposive
constructions, *zhao* ' find, look for (someone) ' is the only V1 used
with *tan*.

Table 8.7 Collocations of V1 with V2 (frequency > 7) in purposive constructions

V1		V2	
posture or change of posture (either head or body) verbs	**14**		**27**
tai (or hui) tou 'raise (or turn) one's head'	7		
zhan 'stand'	3		
zuo 'sit'	1	*kan* 'look, watch'	
zhuan shen 'turn one's body'	1		
zhuanguo lian 'turn over one's face'	1		
ting zhu 'stop moving, stand still'	1		
other verb types (frequency = 1):	13		
zhao 'find, look for, search'	3	*qu* 'go'	**20**
zuo 'sit, take (vehicle)'	2		
xiang 'think'	2		
other verb types (frequency = 1):	13		
verbs with *hui* 'meeting' or its compound as an object:	**4**	*yanjiu* 'study, do research, discuss'	**10**
zhuchi (huiyi) 'chair (the meeting)'	1		
zhaokai (dahui) 'hold (a big meeting)'	1		
kai (hui) 'hold (a meeting)'	1		
zuzhi zhaokai (dahui) 'organize and hold (a big meeting)'	1		
lai 'come'	3		
jiehe 'combine, unite'	2		
canjia 'participate in'	1		
yongdao 'use to'	2	*xuexi* 'study'	10
tou 'throw'	2		
other verb types (frequency = 1):	6		
verb phrases with *qian* 'money' as the object:	**8**	*mai* 'buy'	10
hua (qian) 'spend (money)'	6		
gei (qian) 'give (somebody money)'	1		
fu 'pay (money)'	1		
other verb types (frequency = 1):	2		

续表

V1		V2	
zhao 'find, look for, search'	2	*zuo* 'do,	9
jian 'cut'	2	make'	
other verb types (frequency = 1) :	5		
nazhe 'take, carry'	2	*lai* 'come'	9
zhengzhe 'compete for'	2		
dai 'carry, take'	2		
other verb types (frequency = 1) :	3		
kai (*kou*) 'open one's mouth'	2	*shuo* (*ming*)	8
other verb types (frequency = 1) :	6	'say, explain'	

In purposive constructions, some verbs such as motion verbs (*lai* 'come' and *qu* 'go'), the verb *zhao* 'find, look for, search', and the verb *mai* 'buy' can easily enter into this kind of construction either as V1 or V2 or both (in the case of *qu* 'go'). On average, out of ten verb tokens, there are five verb types used in either the V1 or the V2 position.

8.4 *Shared Object Construction*

Some linguists (e. g. Baker 1989) claim that the shared object construction is the only ture type of serial verb construction. However, shared object constructions are not common at all in Mandarin Chinese. Examples in (194) are from the LCMC.

(194)a. (*wo*)　*gei*　　　*ta*　　**mai** *ji*　　*ke*　*tang*　**chi**

　　　(I)　　give, for 3SGM　buy　a few　CL　candy　**eat**

　　　' (I) ...buy a few candies for him to eat'

　　b. (*ta*)　　　*jiu*　**zhao**　　　*cankao*　　*shu*　　**kan**

(3SGF)   just   **look. for**   reference   book   **read**

'(she) just looked for reference books to read'

There are only 21 instances of shared object constructions from my search of the LCMC. In shared object constructions, two verbs share the same overt object which shows up intervening between the two verbs. The two sub-events denoted by V1 and V2 bear a tight purposive relationship. Table 8.8 displays the frequency of V1 and V2 for these 21 cases.

Table 8.8   Frequency of V1 and V2 for shared object constructions

V1	Freq	V2	Freq
you ' have, there be'	7	*chi* ' eat'	**10**
cooking verbs:	5	*kan* ' look'	3
shao ' cook'	3	*chansheng* ' produce, make'	2
chao ' fry'	1	*baogao* ' report'	2
lao ' bake in a pan'	1	*jue* ' chew'	1
mai ' buy'	3	*nian* ' twist with fingers'	1
zhao ' look for, find'	2	*gei* ' give'	1
dai ' take'	1	*jiang* ' tell, speak'	1
zhua ' catch'	1		
wa ' dig'	1		
bei ' fetch by carrying on the back'	1		
Total	21		21

In the V1 position of shared object constructions, *you* ' have, there be' and verbs which denote cooking are quite common. In the V2 position, there is one verb *chi* ' eat', which stands out, and it is very frequently used as V2, as Table 8.9 shows.

Table 8.9   Collocations of V1 verbs with *chi* as V2

V1	Freq	V2	Freq
cooking verbs:	5	*chi* ' eat '	**10**
shao ' cook '	3		
chao ' fry '	1		
lao ' bake in a pan '	1		
obtaining by means:	5		
mai ' buy '	2		
zhao ' look for, find '	1		
wa ' dig '	1		
beilai ' fetch by carrying on the back '	1		

For the verb *chi* ' eat ' as V2, there are 5 instances of V1 which denote cooking and another 5 verbs which denote the concept of obtaining something by buying, finding, digging or fetching. It seems that it is a common phenomenon that first we should cook something or obtain something in various ways in order for us to eat it later. In fact, all the ten instances of *chi* ' eat ' used as V2 have the collocating verbs either denoting cooking or denoting obtaining by some means. In shared object constructions, both V1 and V2 are not quite free and V2 is even more restricted. The verb *chi* ' eat ' makes up about 50% of all the verbs in the V2 position.

8.5 *Compound Construction*

In multi-verb constructions, compound constructions are very frequent. In the search results, there are 861 cases of compound constructions, most of which involve motion verbs. Table 8.10 shows the frequency and percentage of compounds with motion verbs and those without motion verbs. First, I would like to discuss compounds which contain motion verbs.

Table 8.10   Compounds with motion verbs and those without motion verbs

Total number: 861	With motion verbs	Without motion verbs
Frequency	679	182
Percentage	79%	31%

Among the 679 verb compounds containing motion verbs to indicate results or directions, there are 646 instances of contiguous compounds in which there are no intervening elements between their constituents and 33 non-contiguous compounds in which there are some intervening elements within the compounds. Li and Thompson (1981) claim that some directional VV compounds allow their objects to intervene between the two verbs to form split (non-contiguous) compounds as in *na shu chulai* ' take (the) book exit come - take (the) book out '. Discussions of compounds in this section will be mainly devoted to contiguous compounds with motion verbs since such compounds are typical and the most frequent type of compound constructions. Table 8.11 displays the frequency of V1 and V2 (Freq ⩾ 3) in these 646 cases of contiguous compounds with motion verbs.

A motion verb can be the first constituent or the second constituent of a compound. However, if there is a motion verb in a VV compound, it usually takes up the V2 position. From Table 8.11, it can be seen that the two most frequent verbs used as V1 are the motion verbs *zou* ' walk ' and *dai* ' bring, take '. The two most frequent verbs in the V2 positions are *qilai* ' rise come ', which is commonly used to express aspectual meanings and *chulai* ' exit come - come out ', which is mostly used to express results. Other motion verbs used commonly as V2 are *lai* ' come ', *dao* ' reach, get to ', *qilai* ' rise (come) ', *qu* ' go ' and *chu* ' exit '. Table 8.11 indicates that in VV compounds containing motion verbs, V1 is more open for verb types than V2 while V2 is much more restricted.

Table 8.11   Frequency of V1 and V2 (F ≥ 3) for compounds with motion verbs

Freq	V1	Freq	V2 (motion verbs)	Freq
Over 100			*qilai* ' rise (come) '	**143**
			chulai ' come out '	**102**
26—100	*zou* ' walk '	57	*lai* ' come '	**73**
	dai ' bring, take '	27	*dao* ' reach, get to '	**73**
			qu ' go '	**61**
			chu ' exit '	**46**
10—25	*zuo* ' sit '	22	*shang* ' ascend, go up '	24
	chi ' eat '	20	*xialai* ' come down '	21
	zhao ' search, find '	19	*zou* ' walk leave '	15
	zhan ' stand '	18	*xiaqu* ' go down '	12
	hui ' return '	15	*guolai* ' cross, go over '	11
	xiao ' smile, laugh '	15		
	jiao ' shout, call '	13		
	kan ' look '	12		
	xie ' write '	10		
6—9	*xiang* ' think, want '	9	*qi* ' rise '	8
	shuo ' say '	8	*xia* ' descend, go down '	8
	ting ' listen '	8	*huilai* ' come back '	7
	chu ' exit '	8	*jin* ' enter '	6
	jin ' enter '	8		
	gan ' feel '	7		
	mai ' buy '	7		
	da ' beat, call '	7		
	shi ' lose '	6		
	ku ' cry '	6		
	guo ' cross '	6		

续表

Freq	V1	Freq	V2 (motion verbs)	Freq
4—5	*song* 'send'	5	*guoqu* 'go over'	5
	qing 'ask'	5	*hui* 'return'	5
	hua 'draw'	5	*huiqu* 'go back'	4
	zhan occupy	4	*jinqu* 'go in'	4
	shou 'receive'	4		
	chansheng 'produce, make'	4		
		4		
	pao 'run'	4		
	jiang 'tell speak'	4		
	tiao 'jump'	4		
	tan 'talk'			
Sum of the above		351		**628**
Others (Freq <4)		295		18
Total tokens		646		646

8.5.1 *Contiguous Compounds Containing* Lai 'Come' *and* Qu 'Go'

Most directional compounds contain the motion verb *lai* 'come' or *qu* 'go' or smaller compounds with *lai* 'come' or *qu* 'go' as their constituents. In fact, all the larger directional compounds which take smaller compounds as their constituents contain *lai* 'come' or *qu* 'go' in their final slots. Since these smaller compounds or complements usually do not denote motion any longer but function more like a kind of grammatical marker, they are often listed as single units in grammar books or dictionaries. As illustrated in Table 8.12, Li and Thompson (1981) claim that the motion verb *lai* 'come' or *qu* 'go' can combine with other 7 directional motion verbs to form bi-morphemic complements, which in turn can form tri-morphemic compounds when they are combined with another verb.

Table 8.12   Combination of *lai* 'come' or *qu* 'go' with other seven directional motion verbs to form bi-morphemic compounds

	jin 'enter, in'	chu 'exit, out'	hui 'return, back'	guo 'cross, over'	qi 'rise, up'	shang 'ascend, up'	xia 'descend, down'
lai	jinlai 'enter come'	chulai 'exit come'	huilai 'return come'	guolai 'cross come'	qilai 'rise come'	shanghai 'ascend come'	xialai 'descend come'
qu	jinqu 'enter go'	chuqu 'exit go'	huiqu 'return go'	guoqu 'cross go'	*qiqu 'rise go'	shangqu 'ascend go'	xiaqu 'descend go'

In fact, not all these combinations are possible as Li and Thompson (1981) claimed. Clearly they have not checked the validity of all these combinations against actual language data (Xiao & McEnery 2004). Xiao & McEnery (2004) claim that the combination *qi* 'rise' with *qu* 'go' (*qiqu* 'rise go') is not possible. As displayed in Table 8.13, *qiqu* 'rise go' is missing from the search results of the LCMC.

Table 8.13   Frequency of *lai* 'come' and *qu* 'go' and their combinations with other seven directional motion verbs used as complements in compounds

Pinyin	Gloss	Freq	Pinyin	Gloss	Freq
lai	'come'	73	qu	'go'	61
qilai	'rise come'	143	*qiqu	'rise go'	0
chulai	'exit come'	102	chuqu	'exit go'	2
xialai	'descend come'	21	xiaqu	'descend go'	12
guolai	'cross come'	11	guoqu	'cross go'	5
huilai	'return come'	7	huiqu	'return go'	4
jinlai	'enter come'	3	jinqu	'enter go'	4
shanglai	'ascend come'	2	shangqu	'ascend go'	2
lai total	come (in the final Verb position)	362	qu total	go (in the final Verb position)	90

The directional constituents in contiguous compounds "form a closed class and a more or less cohesive unit" (Xiao & McEnery 2004﹕164). They can be simple or complex forms (compounds) with their final positions filled by the directional verb *lai* ' come ' or *qu* ' go '. In the case of *lai*, most of the directional constituents in such compounds take complex forms. However, the pattern in the case of *qu* is reversed; that is, most of the directional constituents take simple forms rather than complex forms, as Figure 8. 3 indicates.

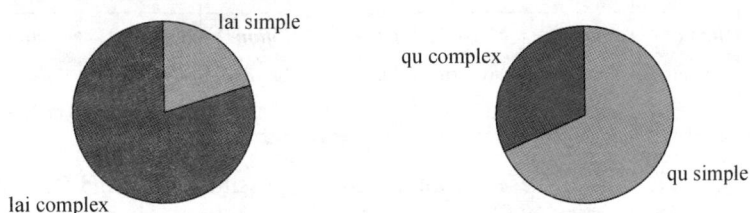

Figure 8. 3　The ratio of the simple and complex forms of *lai* and *qu*

In cases where simple *lai* ' come ' and *qu* ' go ' function as directional complements there is not much difference in their token frequency. However, we can ask whether there are any similarities and differences in the verbs which are compounded with these two directional verbs? Table 8. 14 shows the verbs which collocate with simple *lai* ' come ' and *qu* ' go ' and their frequency.

Table 8. 14　Collocations of verbs with simple *lai* ' come ' and *qu* ' go '

Verb	Verbs collocate with *lai* and *qu*	Freq	Verbs only collocate with *lai*	Freq	Verbs only collocate with *qu*	Freq
lai ' come ' (73)	*dai* ' bring, take '	13	*mai* ' buy '	4		
	zou ' walk, leave '	6	*chuan* ' pass '	2		
	hui ' return, back '	6	*da* ' beat, call '	2		
	chu ' exit, in '	4	*gan* ' hurry '	2		
	zhao ' search, look for '	4	*qi* ' rise '	2		
		3	*hui* ' remit '	1		
	jin ' enter, in '					

续表

Verb	Verbs collocate with *lai* and *qu*	Freq	Verbs only collocate with *lai*	Freq	Verbs only collocate with *qu*	Freq
lai 'come' (73)	*jiao* 'shout, call, ask'	3	*ban* 'move'	1		
	song 'send'	3	*hui* 'return, back'	1		
	ben 'rush'	2	*qing* 'ask'	1		
	guo 'cross'	2	*shang* 'ascend, up'	1		
	fei 'fly'	1	*xia* 'descend, down'	1		
			xie 'write'	1		
			xue 'learn'	1		
			ya 'take into custody'	1		
			yong 'gush'	1		
			cha 'explore'	1		
			zhuan 'make (profit)'	1		
			zhua 'catch'	1		
qu 'go' (61)	*dai* 'bring, take'	3			*shi* 'lose'	6
	zou 'walk, leave'	11			*you* 'swim'	2
	hui 'return, back'	7			*kan* 'look'	2
	chu 'exit, in'	3			*li* 'leave'	2
	zhao 'search, look for'	1			*diao* 'transfer'	1
	jin 'enter, in'	4			*duo* 'grab'	1
	jiao 'shout, call, ask'	1			*kang* 'carry (on the shoulder)'	1
	song 'send'	2			*pao* 'run'	1
	ben 'rush'	4			*sheng* 'save'	1
	guo 'cross'	1			*shi* 'drive'	1
	fei 'fly'				*si* 'tear'	1
					si 'die'	1
					tui 'fade'	1
					yi 'move'	1
					zhuan yi 'turn, move'	1

It can be seen from Table 8. 14 that both *lai* ' come ' and *qu* ' go '
are quite productive in forming compounds with other verbs. Some of the
motion verbs such as *dai* ' bring, take ', *zou* ' walk, leave ' and *hui*
' return, back ' are used more frequently with both *lai* ' come ' and *qu*
' go '. However, some verbs which are used quite frequently with one
directional verb are not very likely to be compounded with the other due
to their semantic (in) compatibility with either of the two directional
verbs. For example, *shi* ' lose ' collocates quite easily with *qu* ' go ' but
not with *lai* ' come '. Once someone has lost something the thing is away
from her/him and it is beyond the person ' s reach at that time.
Therefore, the meaning of losing is quite compatible with the directional
meaning of being away from someone. Naturally, the meaning of *shi*
' losing ' is contradictory with the semantics of *lai* ' come ' which
indicates general motion toward the speaker. On the other hand, *mai*
' buy ' collocates frequently with *lai* ' come ', but not with *qu* ' go '. The
reason is that when one buys something the thing comes into one ' s
possession rather than going away. Thus, the directional verb *lai* ' come '
is more likely than the directional verb *qu* ' go ' to be used with the verb
mai ' buy '.

In terms of complex forms functioning as directional constituents of
these compounds, forms with the directional verb *lai* ' come ' are much
more frequent than those with the directional verb *qu* ' go ', as Figure 8.
4 shows. When the frequency of individual compounds is examined it has
been found that the imbalance of frequency between complex forms of *lai*
' come ' and those of *qu* ' go ' is mainly due to two pairs of compounds.
In Table 8. 13, the frequency of *chulai* ' exit come, come out ' is 102
while the token frequency for *chuqu* ' exit go, go out ' is only 2. The
frequency of *qilai* ' rise come ' is 143, but there are no instances of its
counterpart *qiqu* ' rise go '. Then, why is there so much difference in
frequency between these two pairs of compounds? Explanations for the
imbalance of their frequency are in order.

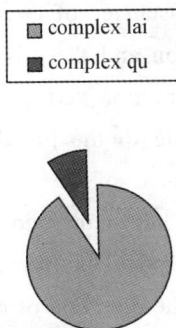

▨ complex lai
■ complex qu

Figure 8.4   Frequency of complex forms of *lai* ' come ' and *qu* ' go '

In Mandarin Chinese, *chulai* ' exit come, come out ' can be used together with real motion verbs or with non-motion verbs. When used with a motion verb this verb specifies the direction of motion. However, when it is compounded with a non-motion verb, it is used idiomatically or metaphorically to "express aspectual meanings such as the result-state and completion/finality of an action" (Xiao & McEnery 2004 : 165). Some examples are given in (195).

(195) a. *Ta   xiang   chulai   yi   ge   hao   zhuyi.*

   3SG think   exit-come one CL   good idea

   ' S/hethought out a good idea. / A good idea occurred to her/him. '

b. *Ta   na   pian   lunwen   xie   chulai   le.*

   S/he   that CL   thesis   write   exit-come PERF

   ' She has finished writing her thesis. ' (Xiao & McEnery 2004 : 165)

In these two sentences, *xiang* ' think ' and *xie* ' write ' obviously are not actual motion verbs and the directional constituent *chulai* ' exit come, come out ' does not indicate a spatial trajectory. It clearly signals the success of obtaining a result. It also adds a telic aspectual meaning to an otherwise atelic verb and implies the completion of the action stated.

Out of 102 occurrences of *chulai* ' exit come, come out ', 49 indicate the direction of real motion, while the remaining 53 cases express an aspectual meaning of signaling the resultative phase of a non-real motion. However, the two instances of *chuqu* 'exit go, go out' both indicate direction of real motion and there is no instance of *chuqu* 'exit go, go out' used with a non-motion verb to indicate a result-state.

Another factor contributing to the imbalance of frequency between complex forms of *lai* and those of *qu* is that there are quite a few instances of *qilai* 'rise come' but there is no instance of *qiqu* 'rise go' in the search results. From the corpus data, it can be seen that *qilai* has three different uses. It can indicate the direction of upward movement (196a) or express the result of an event (196b) or signal the aspectual meaning of inceptiveness (196c), as the examples from the LCMC show.

(196) a. *nu   bianji   zhongyu   zhan   le   qilai*
         woman   editor   finally   stand PERF   rise-come
         'the woman editor finally stood up'

   b. *ta   meiyou   xiang   qilai*
      3SGF   not   think   rise-come
      'she could not recall it'

   c. *yushi   ta   tongku   di   ku   le   qilai*
      There fore   s/he   miserably PAR   cry PERF   rise-come
      'therefore, he began to cry miserably'

Most of the instances with *qilai* 'rise come' signal the aspectual meaning of inceptiveness. In such kind of use, *qilai* 'rise come' does not specify direction of real motion but indicate the situation has started and will continue as in the case *ku qilai* 'began to cry'. Here, this directional verb has been extended to function as an aspectual marker. On the other hand, in the search results there is no instance of its counterpart *qiqu* 'rise go' used as an aspectual marker. There is not even an instance of *qiqu* 'rise go' used to indicate a result state of an event.

Mandarin speakers seem to prefer using complex forms of *lai* 'come' rather than *qu* 'go' to indicate a resulting state. As for the inceptive aspectual marker, *qilai* instead of its counterpart *qiqu* 'rise go' has won the race to serve this function and *qilai* is used quite frequently to indicate this aspectual meaning. These are the two important factors to cause the imbalance in frequency between the complex form of *lai* 'come' and that of *qu* 'go'.

8.5.2 Contiguous Compounds Containing Motion Verbs other than Lai and Qu

Many compounds with motion verbs contain simple or complex forms of *lai* or *qu*. Contiguous compounds containing motion verbs other than *lai* and *qu* in V2 slots are also common though their frequency is not as high as that of those containing *lai* and *qu*. Table 8.15 reflects the frequency of individual verbs for these compounds with motion verbs other than *lai* and *qu* in the V2 position.

Talmy (2000) terms the path or directional verbs in Table 8.15 as satellites. In Chinese, certain verbs, typically verbs of displacement (e. g. , *hui* 'return' , *zou* 'walk' , *guo* 'cross') and dislocation (e. g. , *na* 'take' , *ban* 'remove') can serve as the main verbs (V1) in directional verbal compounds. Many of these verbs conflate movement with some other activity such as manner or cause. The satellites usually denote path or direction. The prototypical satellite verbs functioning as directional complements in VV compounds are *lai* 'come' and *qu* 'go', which have been discussed previously. However, as illustrated in Table 8.15 there is a set of additional verbs, which can also serve as complements of direction or result-states.

Table 8.15   Frequency of motion verbs other than *lai* and *qu* in MVCs

Pinyin	Gloss	Freq	Pinyin	Gloss	Freq
shang	'ascend, up'	24	*xia*	'descend, down'	8
chu	'exit, out'	46	*jin*	'enter, in'	6
dao	'get to, reach, to'	73	*zou*	'walk, leave, away'	15
qi	'rise'	8	*hui*	'return'	5
diao	'drop, away'	3	*dai*	'bring, take'	2
zhi	'reach, to'	1	*dong*	'move, be able to'	1
guo	'cross, over'	1	*pao*	'run (away)'	1
Total		194			

The motion verb *dao* '*get to*, *reach*, *arrive*' is used frequently as a complement (satellite) in VV compounds. Table 8. 16 reflects the collocated verbs used with *dao*.

Table 8. 16   Frequency of collocated verbs used with *dao*

Freq of V1				V2
Sense Verbs:	22	**Communication Verbs:**	11	*dao*, get
gan(*jue*, *shou*) 'feel'	9	*shuo* 'tell, speak'	3	to,
kan 'look'	8	*tan* 'speak'	3	reach,
ting 'listen'	3	*jiao*, 'call'	3	arrive
jian 'see'	1	*qing* 'ask, invite'	2	
pie 'have a glimpse'	1			
Searching Verb:	7	**Cognition Verbs:**	5	
zhao 'search look for'	6	*xiang* 'think'	2	
xunzhao 'search, look for'	1	*lian xiang* 'think by associations'	1	
		ling shou 'get to know'	1	
Others:	28	*renshi* 'realize'	1	
shou 'receive'	4			
zhan 'occupy, take up'	4			
chi 'eat'	3			
da 'reach'	3			
de 'get, obtain'	3			
lai 'come'	2			
chengshu 'ripen'	1			
dai 'take'	1			
fen 'divide'	1			
hui 'return'	1			
kai 'drive'	1			
mai 'buy'	1			
shi 'pick up'	1			
song 'send'	1			
zhuo 'pick up by mouth'	1			

Table 8. 16 shows that verbs of senses, communication, searching and recognition collocate commonly with *dao*. The total token frequency for these 4 types of verb is 45, which takes up 61. 6% out of the 73 instances. The most frequent verb type used with *dao* is verbs of senses (including its metaphorical use such as *gan* 'feel, realize').

In Chinese, unlike in English, some verbs often do not specify the results by themselves. It is often the satellites (in Talmy's terms) that achieve this function of specifying the result-state. With *dao* being used together with these verbs, the results are signalled. For example, when *ting* 'listen' is used with *dao* 'reach, get to', the resulting compound is interpreted as hear something (the result of the action of listening has been achieved).

As Table 8.15 indicates, the next most frequently used satellite in its simple form is *chu* 'exit, out'. Compared with the frequency of *chu*, the frequency of its counterpart is quite low and there are only six cases of *jin* 'enter, in'. The collocating verbs with *chu* 'exit, out' and those with *jin* 'enter, in' are illustrated in Table 8.17.

Table 8.17 Frequency of collocating verbs with *chu* and *jin* as V2

Freq of collocating verbs with *chu* (46)		Freq of collocating verbs with *jin* (6)	
xie 'write'	8	*xie* 'write'	1
zou 'walk'	5	*na* 'take'	1
zhao 'search'	5	*ting* 'listen'	1
chansheng 'produce'	4	*da* 'fight'	1
shuo 'say, speak'	4	*zuo* 'sit'	1
chou 'pull'	4	*zhuang* 'knock'	1
ting 'listen'	2		
dai 'take'	1		
fazhan 'develop'	1		
gong 'tell'	1		
jiang 'tell'	1		
jiao 'call'	1		
kua 'step'	1		
mai 'sell'	1		
na 'take'	1		
qing 'ask'	1		
qu 'take'	1		
xianlu 'appear'	1		
xiang 'think'	1		
xiao 'laugh'	1		
tan 'probe'	1		

The three verbs *xie* 'write', *na* 'take' and *ting* 'listen' collocate with both *chu* and *jin* in the table. In the forty-seven instances of *chu* from the search results, most of them (33 out of 47) are used to indicate the result-state and there are fourteen cases which specify direction. Out of the six cases involving *jin*, 'enter, in', four indicate direction of real motion. The remaining two signal abstract path (*ting jin* 'listen in accept (the advice)'; *xie jin xiao shuo* 'write into the novel') and none of them indicates the result-state. It seems that the frequency imbalance between *chu* and *jin* is chiefly due to the fact that Chinese prefers *chu* to *jin* to indicate the result-state. The preference may be related to their respective semantics of these two verbs.

In compound constructions which have been just discussed, there is an obvious asymmetry between V1 and V2 in the way that the V1 slot draws its verbs from a larger lexical pool while verbs in the V2 slot is much more restricted. In these compounds, V2 mostly functions as a kind of directional or resultative marker. Compound constructions in which one verb is usually completely incorporated into another exemplify the highest degree of event integration among MVCs.

Chapter Nine

Conclusions

My classification for an SVC in Mandarin is based on the three iconically based semantic principles: **temporal sequence** and **scope**, **shared participants**, and **situational dependence**. Grounded on these three principles, seven morphosyntactic and prosodic tests have been proposed in this study to apply to the 5 constructions. The application of these tests indicates that coordinate clause constructions and clausal complement constructions are more likely to be interpreted as involving separate events, while purposive complement constructions, double-headed constructions and VV compound constructions are generally construable as two causally connected phases of a single event. The five constructions reflect degrees of serialization or event conflation in Mandarin. Consequently, a continuum of event (in) dependence unifies constructions like (3), in which two VPs denote simple temporal or purposive interdependence; constructions like (4), in which two VPs share an object; and constructions like (5), in which two verbs are compounded to denote a single event conceptually. A construction like (1) represents the limiting case of complete event autonomy on one end, while the one in (5) represents the limiting case of complete event conflation on the other (cf. Langacker 1991, Chapter 10).

This monograph has argued that the main differences between SVCs and non-SVCs are best understood in term of profiling. Both events are considered to be both profiled in the case of coordination and serialization, since both events are raised to a distinctive level of prominence in these two constructions. However, the relation between the two profiled events differs in coordination and serialization. The two profiled events in a typical coordinate construction are independent and there is only a weak semantic relation between them. The two profiled events in the serialization construction are semantically inter-dependent and are typically construed as two phases of one larger "macro event". In the case of subordination, only one event is profiled while the secondary event is usually expressed as a case of complementation or modification.

The corpus results indicate that there is a delicate interaction between lexical items and the construction types they enter into. The results also suggest that there are degrees of freedom and fixedness in the collocating verbs associated with different multi-verb constructions. In coordinate clauses, V1 and V2 are almost completely free lexically and virtually any kind of verb can be inserted in either position. Usually we cannot discern any situational dependence between the two VPs or the events they designate. In clausal complements, V1 is lexically restricted, being mainly inceptive or psychological verbs, while V2is quite open. In purposive constructions, the V1 and V2positions are relatively free but the two verbs should hold some purposive relationship to each other. In shared object constructions, both V1 and V2 are mainly action and transitive verbs. They act on or affect the same participant. A tight purposive relationship can be found between two verbs in this construction. In compound constructions, V1 is relatively open while V2 are quite restricted lexically and they are either phase/achievement verbs or motion verbs.

In order to provide supporting evidence for the degree of event (in) dependence suggested by the seven morphosyntactic tests, a psycholinguistic study was developed whereby native speakers of Mandarin performed a variety of tasks on the ratings of complex sentences, including the five sentence types given above. The experimental results, like the phenomena themselves, provided evidence for a kind of iconicity operating in the coding of multi-verb structures in Mandarin. In so doing, I demonstrated, like so many cognitive linguists have done, that many linguistic units are of a graded phenomenon and that conceptualization has an effect on, if not distinctive grammatical structure, then distinctive grammatical interpretation.

Bibliography

Agbedor, Paul. 1994. Verb serialization in Ewe. *Nordic Journal of African Studies*, 3, 1: 115-135.

Aikhenvald, Alexandra Y. & R. M. W. Dixon (eds.). 2006. *Serial verb constructions: A cross-linguistic typology*. Oxford, U. K. & New York: Oxford University Press.

Aikhenvald, Alexandra Y. 2006. Serial verb constructions in typological perspective. In Alexandra Y. Aikhenvald & R. M. W. Dixon (eds.), *Serial verb constructions: A cross-linguistic typology*, 1-68. Oxford, U. K. & New York: Oxford University Press.

Baker, Mark C. 1989. Object sharing and projection in serial verb constructions. *Linguistic Inquiry*, 20, 4: 513-53.

_____. 1991. On the relation of serialization to verb extensions. In Claire Lefebvre (ed.), *Serial verbs: Grammatical, comparative and cognitive approaches*, 79-102. Amsterdam & Philadelphia: John Benjamins.

Bamgbose, Ayo. 1974. On serial verbs and verbal status. *Journal of West African Languages*, 9, 1: 17-48.

Berman, R. A., & D. I. Slobin. 1994. *Relating events in narrative: A crosslinguistic developmental study*. Hillsdale, N. J. : Lawrence Erlbaum Associates.

Bybee, Joan L. 1988. Morphology as lexical organization. In Michael Hammond & Michael Noonan (eds.), *Theoretical morphology: Approaches in Modern Linguistics*, 119-41. San Diego: Academic

Press.

Bybee, Joan L. & Paul Hopper. 2001. Introduction to frequency and the emergence of linguistic structure. In Joan L. Bybee & Paul Hopper (eds.), *Frequency and the emergence of linguistic structure*, 1-24. Amsterdam: John Benjamins.

Campbell, Richard. 1992. Serial verbs and unaccusativity. *MIT Working Papers in Linguistics*, 17: 41-51.

Chan, Alice Yin Wa. 1997. Temporal sequence and Chinese serial verb constructions. Paper presented at the Ninth North American Conference on Chinese Linguistics. University of Victoria, Canada.

_____. 1998. Formal criteria for interpreting Chinese serial verb constructions. *Communications of COLIPS*, 8, 1: 13-29.

_____. 1999. Notes on the classifications of Chinese serial verb constructions. *Journal of the Chinese Language Teachers Association*, 34, 1: 1-20.

_____. 2000. Chinese serial verb constructions with experiential aspect marker-syntactic representations and semantic interpretations. *Communications of COLIPS*, 10, 1: 69-97.

_____. 2002. Syntactic structures of Chinese serial verb constructions. *Journal of Chinese Linguistics*, 30, 1: 16-38.

Chang, Claire Hsun-huei. 1990. On serial verbs in Mandarin Chinese: VV compounds and Co-Verbal Phrases. *Ohio State University Working Papers in Linguistics*, 39: 316-339.

Chang, Lili. 2003. Verb compounding and iconicity. *Language and Linguistics*, 4, 1: 1-27.

Chao, Yuen Ren. 1968. *A Grammar of spoken Chinese*. Berkeley: University of California Press.

Chen, H. C. (ed.). 1997. *Cognitive processing of Chinese and related Asian Languages*. Hong Kong: The Chinese University Press.

Chen, Xilong. 1993. *On the syntax of serial verb constructions in Chinese*. PhD dissertation. University of Georgia.

Cheng, Jianming. 1986. *On sentence types of modern Chinese*. Beijing: Language Publishing Press.

Chomsky, Noam. 1957. *Syntactic structures*. The Hague & Paris: Mouton.

_____. 1965. *Aspects of the theory of syntax*. Cambridge, Mass. : MIT Press.

_____. 1982. *Some concepts and consequences of the theory of government and binding*. Cambridge, Mass. : MIT Press.

Christaller, Rev. J. G. 1875. *A grammar of the Asante and Fante Language called Tshi*. Basel. Republished 1964. Farmborough, England: P. Gregg.

Chung, Samuel. 1994. *A practical Chinese grammar*. Hong Kong: The Chinese University of Hong Kong.

Collins, Chris. 1997. Argument sharing in serial verb constructions. *Linguistic Inquiry*, 28, 3: 461-497.

Comrie, Bernard. 1976. *Aspect: An introduction to the study of verbal aspect and related problems*. Cambridge: Cambridge University Press.

Coseriu, Eugenio. 1974. *Synchrony, diachrony and history*. Munich: Fink.

Croft, William. 2001. *Radical construction grammar: Syntactic theory in typological perspective*. Oxford, U. K. & New York: Oxford University Press.

Croft, William & D. Alan Cruse. 2004. *Cognitive linguistics*. Cambridge: Cambridge University Press.

Dai, John Xiang-ling. 1990. Syntactic constructions in serial verb expressions in Chinese. *Ohio State University Working Papers in Linguistics*, 39: 316-339.

_____. 1997. Syntactic, morphological and phonological words in Chinese, in J. Packard (ed.), *New Approaches to Chinese Word Formation: Morphology, phonology and the lexicon in modern and ancient Chinese*, 103-134. (*Trends in Linguistics Studies and Monographs* 105.) Berlin & New York: Mouton de Gruyter.

Dai, Y. *A study of Aspect of Modern Chinese*. Hangzhou, China: Zhejiang Eductional Press.

De Francis, John. 1984. *The Chinese language: Facts and fantasy*. Honolulu: University of Hawaii Press.

Fagerli, Ole Torfinn. Malefactive by means of give. 2001. In H. G. Simonsen, & R. T. Endresen (eds.), *A cognitive approach to the verb: Morphological and constructional perspectives*, 203-222. Berlin & New York: Mouton de Gruyter.

Fillmore, Charles, Paul Kay & Catherine O'Connor. 1988. Regularity and idiomaticity in grammatical constructions: The case of *let alone*. *Language*, 64: 501-38.

Fillmore, Charles. 1997. *Santa Cruz lectures on deixis*. Stanford, CA. : CSLI Publications.

Foley, William A. & Robert D. Van Valin, Jr. 1984. *Functional syntax and universal grammar*. Cambridge: Cambridge University Press.

Frawley, William. 1992. *Linguistic semantics*. Hillsdale, N. J. : Lawrence Erlbaum Associates.

Gao, Qiao. 1997. Resultative verb compounds and BA-construction in Chinese. *Journal of Chinese Linguistics*, 25, 1: 84-130.

Giddens, Anthony. 1977. *Studies in social and political theory*. London: Hutchinson.

Goldberg, Adele E. 1995. *Constructions: A construction grammar approach to argument structure*. Chicago: University of Chicago Press.

_____. 2003. Constructions: A new theoretical approach to language. *Trends in Cognitive Science*, 7: 219-224.

_____. 2006. *Constructions at work: The nature of generalization in language*. Oxford, U. K. & New York: Oxford University Press.

Gries, Stefan Th. 2003. Towards a corpus-based identification of prototypical instances of constructions. *Annual Review of Cognitive Linguistics*, 1 : 1-27.

Gries, Stefan Th & Anatol Stefanowitsch. 2006. *Corpora in cognitive linguistics : Corpus-based approaches to syntax and lexis.* Berlin & New York : Mouton de Gruyter.

Grimshaw, Jane B. 1990. *Argument structure.* Cambridge, Mass. : MIT Press.

Givón, Talmy. 1991. Some substantive issues concerning verb serialization : grammatical vs. cognitive packaging. In Claire Lefebvre (ed.) , *Serial verbs : Grammatical, comparative and cognitive approaches*, 137-184. Amsterdam & Philadelphia : John Benjamins.

Gross, Maurice. 1979. On the failure of generative grammar. *Language*, 55 : 859-885.

Haiman, John. 1983. Iconic and economic motivation. *Language*, 59 : 781-819.

_____ (ed.) 1985. *Iconicity in syntax.* Amsterdam & Philadelphia : John Benjamins.

_____ . 1991. Motivation, repetition and emancipation : The bureaucratisation of language. In H. Christoph Wolfart (ed.) , *Linguistic studies presented to John L. Finlay*, 45-70. Algonquian and Iroquoian Linguistics (Winnipeg, Manitoba).

_____ . 1994. Ritualization and the development of language. In William Pagliuca (ed.) , *Perspectives on grammaticalization*, 3-28. Amsterdam : John Benjamins.

Harrison, C. J. 1992. *The grammar of directional serial verb constructions in Thai.* Honours dissertation. Australian National University.

Her, One-Soon. 1990. Historical development of *ba* and *jiang* in the Tang Dynasty. *Language Variation and Change*, 2, 3 : 277-294

Hopper, Paul. 1987. Emergent grammar. *Proceedings of the Annual Meeting of the Berkeley Linguistic Society*, 13 : 139-157.

_____ . 1988. Emergent Grammar and the A Priori Grammar Postulate. In D. Tannen (ed.), *Linguistics in Context*, 117-134. Norwood, N. J. : Ablex.

_____. 1998. Emergent Grammar. In M. Tomasello (ed.), *The New Psychology of Language*, 155-175. Mahwah, N. J. : Lawrence Erlbaum Associates.

Hopper, Paul & S. A. Thompson. 1980. Transitivity in grammar and discourse. *Language*, 56: 251-299.

Hopper, Paul & Elizabeth C. Traugott. 1993. *Grammaticalization*. Cambridge: Cambridge University Press.

Huang, Chu-Ren & Kathleen Ahrens. 1999. The function and category of *gei* in Mandarin ditransitive constructions. *Journal of Chinese Linguistics*, 27, 2: 1-26.

Huang, C. -T. James. 1984. Phrase structure, lexical integrity and Chinese compounds. *Journal of the Chinese Teachers' Association*, 19, 2: 53-48.

Huang, C. -T. James & Audrey Yen-Hui Li (eds.). 1996. *New horizons in Chinese linguistics*. Dordrecht: Kluwer Academic Press.

Hung, Tony T. 1986. *Serial verb constructions in Chinese: A semantic analysis*. UCSD ms.

Hwang, Jya-Lin. 2000. *On grammaticalization in serial verb constructions in Chinese*. PhD dissertation. University of Hawaii.

Ji, Shaojun. 1997. Imperfective verbs and the BA construction: An analysis from the "Transitive Prototype" perspective. *Papers in Experimental and Theoretical Linguistics*, 4: 11-21. University of Alberta.

Kang, Jian. 1999. *The Composition of the perfective aspect in Mandarin Chinese*. PhD Dissertation. Boston University.

Kay, Paul & Charles Fillmore. 1999. Grammatical constructions and linguistic generalizations: the *what's X doing Y?* construction. *Language*, 75: 1-33.

Kemmer, Suzanne & Michael Barlow. 2000. Introduction: A usage-based conception of language. In Michael Barlow & Suzanne Kem-

mer (eds.), *Usage based models of language*, vii-xxvii. Stanford:
CSLI Publications.

Kim, Jeongdal. 1994. *The serial verb construction in Korean*. PhD dissertation. University of Southern California.

Lakoff, George. 1987. *Women, fire, and dangerous things: What categories reveal about the mind*. Chicago: Chicago University Press.

Lakoff, George & Mark Johnson. 1980. *Metaphors we live by*. Chicago & London: University of Chicago Press.

Lamarre, Christine. 2007. The Linguistic Encoding of Motion Events in Chinese: With Reference to Cross-dialectal Variation. In C. Lamarre & T. Ohori (eds.), *Typological Studies of the Linguistic Expression of Motion Events*, Volume 1: *Perspectives from East and Southeast Asia*, 3-33. Tokyo: Center for Evelotionary Cognitive Sciences at the University of Tokyo.

Langacker, Ronald W. 1987. *Foundations of Cognitive Grammar. Vol. 1, Theoretical prerequisites*. Stanford: Stanford University Press.

_____. 1988. A view of linguistic semantics. In Brygida Rudzka-Ostyn (ed.), *Topics in Cognitive Linguistics*, 49-90. Amsterdam: John Benjamins.

_____. 1990. *Concept, image, and symbol: The basis of grammar*. (Cognitive Linguistic Research 1.) Berlin & New York: Mouton de Gruyter.

_____. 1991. *Foundations of Cognitive Grammar. Vol. 2, Descriptive application*. Stanford: Stanford University Press.

_____. 1993. Reference-point constructions. *Cognitive Linguistics*, 4, 1: 1-38.

_____. 1995. Viewing in cognition and grammar. In Philip Davis (ed.), *Alternative linguistics: Descriptive and theoretical modes*, 153-212. (Current Issues in Linguistic Theory 102.) Amsterdam & Philadelphia: John Benjamins.

_____. 1999. *Grammar and conceptualization*. Berlin & New York:

Mouton de Gruyter.

_____. 2000. A dynamic usage-based model. In Michael Barlow & Suzanne Kemmer (eds.), *Usage based models of language*, 1-63. Stanford, CA: CSLI Publications.

_____. 2003. Constructional integration, grammaticalization, and serial verb constructions. *Language and Linguistics*, 4, 2: 251-278.

_____. 2008. *Cognitive grammar: A basic introduction*. Oxford, U. K. & New York: Oxford University Press.

Larson, Richard K. 1991. Some issues in verb serialization. In Claire Lefebvre (ed.), *Serial verbs: Grammatical, comparative and cognitive approaches*, 185-211. Amsterdam & Philadelphia: John Benjamins.

Law, Paul & Tonjes Veenstra. 1992. On empty operators in serial verb constructions. MIT *Working Papers in Linguistics*, 17: 183-203.

Law, Paul. 1996. A note on the serial verb construction in Chinese. *Cahiers de Linguistique - Asie orientale*, 25, 2: 199 -235.

Lee, David. 2001. *Cognitive linguistics: An introduction*. Oxford, U. K. & New York: Oxford University Press.

Lee, Sookhee. 1993. *The syntax and semantics of serial verb constructions*. PhD dissertation. University of Washington.

Lefebvre, Claire. 1991. *Take* serial verb constructions in Fon. In Claire Lefebvre (ed.), *Serial verbs: Grammatical, comparative and cognitive approaches*, 37-78. Amsterdam & Philadelphia: John Benjamins.

Lefebvre, Claire (ed.). 1991. *Serial verbs: Grammatical, comparative and cognitive approaches*. Amsterdam: Benjamins.

Li, Charles N. & Sandra A. Thompson. 1973. Serial verb constructions in Mandarin Chinese: Subordination or coordination? In Claudia Corum, T. Cedric Smith-Stark & Ann Weiser (eds.), *You Take the high node and I'll take the low node: Papers from the Comparative Syntax Festival*, 96-103. Chicago: Chicago Linguistic Society.

_____. 1974a. An explanation of word order change SVO > SOV. *Foundations of Language*, 12, 2: 201-214.

_____. 1974b. Coverbs in Mandarin Chinese: Verbs or prepositions? *Journal of Chinese Linguistics*, 2, 3: 257-278.

_____. 1976. Development of the causative in Mandarin Chinese: Interaction of diachronic process in syntax. In Masayoshi Shibatani (ed.), *The grammar of causative constructions*. New York: Academic Press.

_____. 1981. *Mandarin Chinese: A functional reference grammar*. Berkeley: University of California Press.

Lakoff, George & Mark Johnson. 1980. *Metaphors we live by*. Chicago: Chicago University Press.

Li, Lingan. 1986. *Sentences patterns in Modern Chinese*. Shanghai: Commercial Press.

Li, Yafei. 1991. On deriving serial verb constructions. In Claire Lefebvre (ed.), *Serial verbs: Grammatical, comparative and cognitive approaches*, 103-135. Amsterdam & Philadelphia: John Benjamins.

Lichtenberk, Frantisek. 1991. Semantic change and heterosemy in grammaticalization. *Language*, 67: 475-509.

Lin, Hua. 2001. *A Grammar of Mandarin Chinese*. Munchen, Germany: Lincom Europa.

Liu, Cai-Xia. 1991. The Chinese serial verb construction proper. *Calgary Working Papers in Linguistics*, 14: 85-148.

Lord, Carol. 1982. The development of object markers in serial verb languages. In P. Hopper & S. A. Thompson (eds), *Syntax and semantics* 15, *Studies in transitivity*, 277-299. New York: Academic Press.

_____. 1993. *Historical changes in serial verb constructions*. Amsterdam & Philadelphia: John Benjamins.

Lu, Jiping. 1984. *Complex predicates*. Shanghai: Shanghai Education Publishing Press.

Lu, Shuxiang. 1999. *Eight hundred words in modern Chinese*. Shanghai: Commercial Press.

Matthews, Stephen. 2006. On Serial verb constructions in Cantonese. In Alexandra Y. Aikhenvald & R. M. W. Dixon (eds.), *Serial verb constructions: A cross-linguistic typology*, 69-87. Oxford, U. K. & New York: Oxford University Press.

McCabe, Allyssa. 1998. Sentences combined: Text and discourse. In J. B. Gleason, & N. B. Ratner (eds.), *Psycholinguistics*, 275-308. New York: Harcourt Brace College Publishers.

McEnery, Tony; Richard Xiao & Yukio Tono. 2006. *Corpus-based language studies: An advanced resource book*. London & New York: Routledge.

McEnery, Tony; Zhonghua Xiao & Lili Mo. 2003. Aspect Marking in English and Chinese: Using the Lancaster Corpus of Mandarin Chinese for contrastive language study. *Literary and Linguistic Computing*, 18, 4: 361-378.

Mei, Tsu Lin. 1991. The historical development of the verb-resultative complement construction, with a note on the neutralization of the pre-verbal agent/patient distinction in Middle Chinese. *Yuyanxue luncong*, 16: 112-36.

Newman, John. 1993. The semantics of giving in Mandarin. In Richard A. Geiger, & Brygida Rudzka-Ostyn (eds), *Conceptualizations and mental processing in language*, 433-485. Berlin & New York: Mouton de Gruyter.

_____. 1996. *Give: A cognitive linguistic study*. Berlin & New York: Mouton de Gruyter.

Newman, John & Sally Rice. 2004. Patterns of usage for English SIT, STAND, and LIE: A cognitively inspired exploration in corpus linguistics. *Cognitive Linguistics*, 15, 3: 351-396.

_____. 2006. Transitivity schemas of English EAT and DRINK in the BNC. In S. Th. Gries & A. Stefanowitsch (eds.), *Corpora in*

Cognitive Linguistics: Corpus-based approaches to syntax and lexis, 225-260. Berlin & New York: Mouton de Gruyter.

————. 2008. Asymmetry in English multi-verb sequences: A corpus-based approach. In Barbara Lewandowska-Tomaszczyk (ed.), *Asymmetric events: An interpretation*, 3-22. Amsterdam & New York: John Benjamins.

Newman, John & Jingxia Lin. 2007. The purposefulness of going: A corpus-linguistic study. In J. Walinski, K. Kredens, and S. Gozdz-Roszkowski (eds.), *Corpora and ICT in language studies*, 293-308. Lodz Studies in Language, Vol. 13. Frankfurt am Main: Peter Lang.

Newmeyer, Frederick J. 1992. Iconicity and generative grammar. *Language*, 68: 756-796.

Nishiyama, Kunio. 1998. V-V compounds as serialization. *Journal of East Asian Linguistics*, 7, 3: 175-217.

Norman, Jerry. 1988. *Chinese.* Cambridge: Cambridge University Press.

Nylander, D. K. 1997. Some myths about serial verbs. *South African Journal of African Languages*, 17, 3: 85-88.

Ochs, Elinor, Emanuel A. Schegloff & Sandra A. Thompson (eds.). 1996. *Interaction and grammar.* Cambridge: Cambridge University Press.

Osam, Emmanuel Kweku. 1994. Review article: Historical change in serial verb constructions. *Journal of African Languages and Linguistics*, 15, 2: 205-210.

Packard, J. (ed.). 1997. *New approaches to Chinese word formation: Morphology, phonology and the lexicon in modern and ancient Chinese.* (Trends in Linguistics Studies and Monographs 105.) Berlin and New York: Mouton de Gruyter.

Packard, J. 2000. *The morphology of Chinese: A linguistic and cognitive approach.* Cambridge: Cambridge University Press.

Pandharipande, Rajeshwari. 1990. Serial verb construction in Marathi. *Ohio State University Working Papers in Linguistics*, 39: 178-199.

Paul, Waltraud. 2004. The "serial verb construction" in Chinese: A Gordian knot. La notion de 《construction verbale en série》 est-elle opératoire? Fédération TUL Atelier du 9 décembre 2004, 1-23. Ehess, Paris.

Peyraube, Alain. 1996. Recent Issues in Chinese Historical Syntax. In C. -T. James Huang & Y. -H. Audrey Li (eds.) , *New horizons in Chinese linguistics*, 161-213. Dordrecht, Netherlands: Kluwer.

Poteet, Stephen R. 1988. *The syntax and semantics of Mandarin coverbs*. UCSD ms.

Pullum, Geoffrey K. 1990. Constraints on intransitive quasi-serial verb constructions in modern colloquial English. *Ohio State University Working Papers in Linguistics*, 39: 218-239.

Rice, Sally. 1987a. *Toward a cognitive model of transitivity*. PhD dissertation. University of California, San Diego.

_____. 1987b. Toward a transitive prototype: Evidence from some a-typical English passive. *Proceedings of the Annual Meeting of the Berkeley Linguistic Society*, 13: 422-434.

Schiller, Eric. 1990a. On the definition and distribution of serial verb constructions. *Ohio State University Working Papers in Linguistics*, 39: 34-64.

_____. 1990b. *An autolexical account of subordinating serial verb constructions*. PhD dissertation. University of Chicago.

Schmid, Hans-Jörg. 2000. *English abstract nouns as conceptual shells: From corpus to cognition*. Berlin & New York: Mouton de Gruyter.

_____. (in press). Does frequency in text instantiate entrenchment in the cognitive system? In Glynn Dylan & Kerstin Fischer (eds.) , *Quantitative methods in cognitive semantics*. Berlin: Mouton de Gruyter.

Sebba, Mark. 1987. *The syntax of serial verbs*. Amsterdam & Philadelphia: John Benjamins.

Seuren, Pieter A. M. 1990. Serial verb constructions. *Ohio State University Working Papers in Linguistics*, 39: 14-33.

Shen, Y. M. 1995. The semantics of the Chinese verb "come". In Eugene H. Casad (ed.), *Cognitive linguistics in the Redwoods: The expansion of a new paradigm in linguistics*, 507-540. Berlin, Federal Republic Germany: Walter de Gruyter & Co.

Song, Yuzhu. 1992. *Basic knowledge of modern Chinese grammar.* Beijing: LanguagePublishing Press.

Sophana, Srichampa. 1997. Serial verb constructions in Vietnamese. *Mon-Khmer Studies*, 27: 137-144.

Stefanowitsch, Anatol & Stefan Th Gries. 2003. Collostructions: Investigating the interaction of words and constructions. *International Journal of Corpus Linguistics*, 8, 2: 209-242.

Stewart, J. M. 1963. Some restrictions on objects in Twi. *Journal of African Languages*, 2, 2: 145-149.

Stewart, Osamuyimen Thompson. 2001. *The serial verb construction parameter.* New York: Garland Publishing Company.

Sweetser, Eve. 1988. Grammaticalization and semantic bleaching. *Proceedings of the Annual Meeting of the Berkeley Linguistic Society*, 14: 389-405.

_____. 1990. *From etymology to pragmatics: Metaphorical and cultural aspects of semantic structure.* Cambridge: Cambridge University Press.

Sun, Chaofen. 1996. *Word-order change and grammaticalization in the history of Chinese.* Stanford: Stanford University Press.

Sun, Dexuan. 1987. *Lectures on knowledge of Chinese.* Shanghai: Shanghai Education Publishing Press.

Tai, James. 1984. Verbs and times in Chinese: Vendler's four categories. In David Testen, Veena Mishra& JosephDrogo(eds.), *Lexical Semantics*, 288-296. Chicago: Chicago Linguistic Society.

_____. 1985. Temporal sequence and Chinese word order. In J. Haiman (ed.), *Iconicity in Syntax*, 49-72. Amsterdam & Philadelphia: John Benjamins.

Talmy, L. 1985. Lexicalization patterns: Semantic structure in lexical forms. In T. Shopen (ed.), *Language typology and syntactic description*: Vol. 3. *Grammatical categories and lexicon*, 36-149. Cambridge: Cambridge University Press.

_____. 1988. The relation of grammar to cognition. In Brygida Rudzka-Ostyn (ed.), *Topics in cognitive linguistics*, 165-205. (Current Issues in Linguistics Theory 50.) Amsterdam: John Benjamins.

_____. 1991. Paths to realization: A typology of event integration. *Proceedings of the Annual meeting of the Berkeley Linguistic Society*, 17: 182-187. (Supplement onBuffalo Papers in Linguistics 91.)

_____. 2000. *Toward a cognitive semantics*. Cambridge, Mass. : MIT Press.

Taylor, John R. 2002. *Cognitive grammar*. Oxford, U. K. & New York: Oxford University Press.

Traugott, Elizabeth C. 1988. Pragmatic strengthening and grammaticalization. *Proceedings of the Annual Meeting of the Berkeley Linguistics Society*, 14: 406-416.

Tuggy, D. 1988. Nahuatl causative/applicative in cognitive grammar. In Brygida Rudzka-Ostyn (ed.), *Topics in cognitive linguistics*, 587-618. Amsterdam: John Benjamins.

Vandeloise, C. 1984. *Description of space in French*. PhD dissertation, University of California, San Diego.

Van Valin, Robert D. & Randy J. LaPolla. 1997. *Syntax: Structure, meaning and function*. Cambridge: Cambridge University Press.

Van Voorst, Jan. 1988. *Event structure*. Amsterdam & Philadelphia: John Benjamins.

Wang, Li. 1958. *Hanyu Shigao II* (A draft history of Chinese Grammar). Beijing: Kexue Chubanshe.

Westermann, Diedrich. 1930. *A study of the Ewe language*. London: Oxford University Press.

Williams, Wayne. 1976. Serial verb construction in Krio. *Studies in African Linguistics*, 2: 47-65.

Winford, Donald. 1990. Serial verb constructions and motion events in Caribbean English Creoles. *Ohio State University Working Papers in Linguistics*, 39: 109-148.

Xiao, Richard & Tony McEnery. 2004. *Aspect in Mandarin Chinese: A corpus-based study*. (Studies in Language Companion Series 73.) Amsterdam: John Benjamins.

Yin, Hui. 2001. Event integration and serial verb constructions in Mandarin Chinese. Paper presented at the 7th International Cognitive Linguistics Conference, University of California, Santa Barbara.

_____. 2003a. Why *Na* grammaticalized as instrument marker while *Ba* as object marker. *Proceedings of the 15th North American Conference on Chinese Linguistics*, 504-520. GSIL Publications, University of Southern California.

_____. 2003b. A cognitive account of Mandarin coverbs. *Proceedings of the 2003 Northwest Linguistics Conference*, 201-208. University of Victoria, Canada.

_____. 2005. Grammaticalization of Mandarin transfer verbs *gei* and *bei* as passive markers. In Marie-Odile Junker, Martha McGinnis & Yves Roberge (eds.), *Proceedings of the 2004 Canadian Linguistics Association Conference*, 12 pages. University of Manitoba, Canada.
http://www. chass. utoronto. ca/ ~ cla-acl/actes2004/Yin-CLA-2004. pdf

_____. 2008. Serial verb constructions in English and Chinese. In Milica Radišić(ed.), *Proceedings of the 2007 Canadian Linguistics Association Annual Conference*, 10 pages. University of Saskatchewan, Saskatoon, Canada. http://www. chass. utoronto. ca/ ~ cla-acl/actes2007/Yin. pdf

Yip, Po-Ching & Don Rimmington 1997. *Chinese*: *An essential grammar*. London &New York: Routledge.

————. 1998a. *Basic Chinese*: *A grammar and workbook*. London & New York: Routledge.

————. 1998b. *Intermediate Chinese*. London & New York: Routledge.

Yu, L. M. 1997. *The role of cross-linguistic lexical similarity in the use of motion verbs in English by Chinese and Japanese learners*. PhD dissertation. University of Toronto.

Yusuf, Ore. 1992. On the use of serial verbs. *Research in Yoruba Language and Literature*, 3: 10-29.

Zhang, L. 1995. *A contrastive study of aspectuality in German*, *English and Chinese*. (Berkeley Insights in Linguistics and Semiotics 19.) New York: Peter Lang.

Zhang, Shi. 1990. Correlations between the Double Object Construction and Preposition Stranding. *Linguistic Inquiry*, 21, 2: 312-316.

Zhang, Zhigong. 1959. *Knowledge of Chinese*. Beijing: People's Education Publishing Press.

Zou, Ke. 1994. Directional verb-compounds in Chinese. *Proceedings of the Annual meeting of the Chicago Linguistic Society*, 30: 443-457.

图书在版编目(CIP)数据

以认知理论进行汉语连动式结构的研究/印辉著. —厦门:厦门大学出版社,2012.12
ISBN 978-7-5615-4527-0

Ⅰ.①以… Ⅱ.①印… Ⅲ.①汉语-复杂谓语-语法结构-研究
Ⅳ.①H146.3

中国版本图书馆 CIP 数据核字(2012)第 316104 号

厦门大学出版社出版发行
(地址:厦门市软件园二期望海路 39 号 邮编:361008)
http://www.xmupress.com
xmup@xmupress.com
厦门市明亮彩印有限公司印刷
2012 年 12 月第 1 版 2012 年 12 月第 1 次印刷
开本:889×1194 1/32 印张:6 插页:2
字数:200 千字 印数:1~1 000 册
定价:26.00 元
本书如有印装质量问题请直接寄承印厂调换